Dramatizing Classic Poetry

by Louise Thistle

YOUNG ACTORS SERIES

A Smith and Kraus Book

Dedication

To my father, Lewis Joseph Thistle, who loved acting and the classics
and who taught me to love them too.

A Smith and Kraus Book
Published by Smith and Kraus, Inc.
PO Box 127, Lyme, NH 03768
www.smithandkraus.com

Manufactured in the United States of America

First Edition: September 1999
9 8 7 6 5 4 3 2 1

Book design by Julia Hill Gignoux, Freedom Hill Design
Illustrations by Katrina Cavanaugh, assisted by Emily Packer and Louise Thistle

The Library of Congress Cataloging-In-Publication Data
Thistle, Louise.
Dramatizing classic poetry for middle and high school students / by Louise Thistle. —1st ed.
p. cm. — (Young actors series)
Includes bibliographical references and indexes.
ISBN 1-57525-155-8
1. Drama in education. 2. Poetry—Study and teaching (Elementary)
3. Poetry—Study and teaching (Secondary) I. Title. II. Series.
PN3171.T477 1999
671.39'9—dc21 99-30019
CIP

ISBN-13: 987-1-57525-155-4

Acknowledgments

Imagination! Who can sing thy force?
—Phyllis Wheatley, first Black poet published in English

This book would not have been possible without the help of many people. First, I thank Emily Packer who has spent hundreds of hours with me on every aspect of this book including major editorial and art suggestions. This book in this form would not have been possible without her knowledgeable and creative guidance, encouragement, and support.

I thank Mary Ann Petteway for her expert editorial help. I appreciate the help of Jo Bodinger who edited the manuscript in its initial stages.

Rebecca Beaver field-tested the poems, including performing *Paul Revere's Ride.* She and her students have provided invaluable suggestions for dramatization and questions about literature. Jo Ann Takemoto offered significant advice on the book's organization helping make the material much more accessible to teachers.

Mike Auer gave me helpful ideas on dramatization and literature. He was instrumental in finding teachers in San Diego City schools to field-test the poetry.

I appreciate Kate Wilson's editorial advice, insight into literature, and suggestions for questions about literature that would interest middle-school students. Dianne Tucker-LaPlount gave me ideas on the value of recitation and memorization to develop language and reading. John Lee's enthusiastic recitation of classic poems to my literature class renewed in me the value of reciting memorized poetry.

Dan Toporski continually and graciously offered me help with my computer needs. Norma Slaman and the hosts at the Newbreak Coffee Company in Ocean Beach provided an inviting place to meet. Meigs Ingham, manager of the Old Globe Gift Shop in San Diego, makes my work accessible to teachers.

Matt Vicars helped me research poetry for middle and high school students. Thank you to Fane Wazny for her suggestions on classic poems for upper-grade students to dramatize. Kerry King gave me suggestions on dramatizing *The Jabberwocky* and other poems.

Annie DuBois helped me dramatize *Annabel Lee*. Ann Lyonn-Boutelle suggested scripting Shakespeare's song, *Winter.* Terry Miller shared her students' experience of dramatizing limericks. Marty Ries told me how she would dramatize classic stanzas with students.

Many other teachers have given me feedback, ideas, and invited me into their classrooms to dramatize and perform poetry. Among them are Meijean Chan, Daryl Bade, Lisa Lee, Demetrice Davis, Robin Dime, Cindy Lail, Cory Smith, Sharon Carr, Connie Eitzen, Karen Mann, Beverly Slater, Sandra Lynn Bennett, Bret Harris, Nelly Harris, Irmalee Haffey, Debra Stout, Lorraine Bloomfield, Karen Mann, and Mary Jo Marx.

I must thank Heather Reed, Jean Davis, and the staff of the Ocean Beach branch library for their gracious help with my many book requests. John Vanderby and Evelyn Kooperman of the literature section of the San Diego Library led me to interesting books and helped me with research. Jean Stewart and the staff of the children's section have sent picture books to supplement dramatization. Millie Nelson and Louise Durrant gave me ideas on writing nature poems to dramatize.

The teaching and writing of Sylvan Barnet, my first literature-writing teacher at Tufts University, continue to inspire me. His ability to write in a way to interest and stimulate both college students and literature teachers is remarkable. Jack Sanford continues to offer me valuable insight and writing expertise.

Finally, I thank my husband Charles Francis Dicken who read every word of the manuscript. He gave me important suggestions that have made the writing clearer and better.

Contents

He who reads a poem aloud well is also a poet.
—Ralph Waldo Emerson

PART I: GETTING STARTED

PART II: DRAMATIZING POETRY

To support the ease of integrating dramatization into your literature curriculum, the following format is used for every poem in Chapters 10, 11, 12, and 13.

1. About the Poem

2. Ways to Dramatize

3. Topics for Critical Thinking, Writing, and Art

Part III PERFORMING POETRY

APPENDICES

Introduction

Poetry is the most highly evolved form of speech.
—Joseph Brodsky, Nobel Prize–winning Poet

Dramatizing Classic Poetry is a book for teachers who want to dramatize poetry in the classroom or on stage and who want to integrate dramatization with the study of poems as literature. The poems in the book have been field-tested in classrooms grades six to twelve with students of all socioeconomic and academic backgrounds and English-language abilities.

The book was written to show teachers and students how to dramatize: It provides directions that teachers and students can follow with minimal or no preparation. Many of the poem selections include self-explanatory directions that can be carried out by students with virtually no guidance by teachers.

USING DRAMATIZING CLASSIC POETRY IN THE CLASSROOM

PART ONE, Getting Started, describes how to dramatize poetry in the classroom and on stage and it discusses how to integrate dramatization with the development of language and the study of poems as literature. (Some material in these Chapters is repeated in my other books but is fundamental to the dramatization of literature.) Part One has the following chapters:

CHAPTER 1 describes the three principles of good acting.

CHAPTER 2 explains the four basic principles of effective stage speech and other speaking techniques. This makes the language and imagery come alive to both the participants and an audience.

CHAPTER 3 describes the mechanics of dramatizing poetry, including many ways to dramatize poetry in the classroom and on stage, how to use your classroom as a stage, techniques of memorization, and how to organize students into groups.

CHAPTER 4 explains how to cast and direct students, including how to train the audience in performance methods, how to teach theatre techniques, and how to elicit helpful feedback.

CHAPTER 5 describes how to make and use simple costume pieces, fabrics, props and rhythm instruments.

CHAPTER 6 suggests techniques to develop English language, and it includes examples of poems adapted to this purpose.

CHAPTER 7 provides a model lesson of poetry dramatization using nonsense verse warm-ups to develop speaking and gesture skills. A serious poem, Tennyson's *The Eagle* is dramatized as a little play. The lesson also uses Christina Rossetti's *Caterpillar* to teach students how to dramatize independently in groups.

CHAPTER 8 explains how to choose and adapt poems to dramatize. It also describes how to organize groups to adapt and dramatize poems on their own and how to create your own poetry performance script.

PART TWO, Dramatizing Poetry, is the heart of the book. Each of the five chapters includes poetry of a different type. The types are Limericks, Lyrics, Ballads, Nonsense Verse, and Historical Narrative Poetry.

The poems have been selected for both their dramatic and literary value. Authors included are William Shakespeare, Langston Hughes, Emily Dickinson, Robert Frost, Edgar Allan Poe, Christina Rossetti, William Blake, e. e. cummings, Alfred Lord Tennyson, William Wordsworth, Lewis Carroll, Walt Whitman, Henry Wadsworth Longfellow, Carl Sandburg, Thomas Hardy, Edward Arlington Robinson, and others.

Each poem or group includes an About the Poem synopsis; a section on Ways to Dramatize describing how to introduce the poem; methods to dramatize with the whole class, in pairs and small groups; and ways to stage the poems. Poems often have a cast list, suggested gestures to enact each line, and costume piece and instrument suggestions. All poems are followed by a section on Topics for Critical Thinking, Writing, and Art.

PART THREE is a twenty-five-minute Poetry Performance Script with Nonsense Verse, Limericks, Nature Poetry, Animal Poetry, and a patriotic *America the Beautiful* finale. The script gives all students, in a class of thirty-five, significant roles by including storytellers, actor-reciters, and a sound crew. The performance can be produced in two weeks. It has minimal memorization, and uses simple costume pieces and instruments.

THE APPENDIX contains glossaries of literary and drama terms. It also has an Index of Authors, Titles, and First Lines, an Across the Curriculum Subject Index, and a Selected Bibliography.

Part I

GETTING STARTED

CHAPTER ONE

The Three Principles of Good Acting

Classic acting is larger than life as poetry is larger than life.
—Stanley Kauffmann, theater critic, author

Three simple principles are the foundation of a good acting program:

BELIEVE you are the part you are playing.

Exercise **CONTROL** over your actions and emotions.

Use **VOICE AND MOVEMENT** expressively to portray different characters and their actions and to express the meaning of the words.

These principles are followed by all good actors. If students practice them, their acting will be successful and will improve. Involvement with the literature will be deep and satisfying. Knowing and practicing the principles teaches students about the art of the theatre and can be what makes the experience particularly interesting and rewarding to them.

List these principles on the board or on a chart and refer to them throughout any lesson. If students get off track, it is usually because they are not following one or more of the principles.

BELIEF

Tell students that believing or fully pretending to be the parts they are playing is essential. The more they are able and willing to believe that they are inside the shoes of a character or the fur, feathers, or skin of an animal, the more dynamic and involving the experience will be for them as actors or as audience members. For example, if students are playing menacing ravens, they must climb inside the feathers of that bird with its powerful wings, alert intent eyes, and strong talons. If someone plays an arrogant duchess, she must imagine that she is the center of the universe and deserves instant service.

Everyone acts for a purpose. To create believability, actors should determine what the characters are trying to do in a situation. For example, the epicure in *An Epicure Dining at Crewe* wants to savor exquisite food. The waiter wants the epicure to stop making a fuss. In the poem, *Silver*, the Moon wants to silver the world with her beams and thus needs to fling her beams carefully over every object below.

To inspire belief:

- Discuss with students the need to believe in the parts they're playing to make the drama seem real. Refer to the film, *The Wizard of Oz,* pointing out how seventeen-year-old Judy Garland pretended to be a little girl wanting to get back home to Kansas and how other actors became a wicked witch, a man of tin, a cowardly lion, and a man of straw. This film is a good example because it shows students that adults often act in children's plays.
- Show pictures of the characters or their types and situations to help students climb inside the characters they will play. For example, books depicting the magic of moonlight might help someone play the moon. Pictures of nineteenth-century dandies dining might inspire an actor playing the epicure at Crewe.
- Model belief. For example, when acting the witches' scene in *Macbeth,* stir the brew in the cauldron thoroughly to mix your evil ingredients. Speak in a way to threaten your victim. Cackle to help complete the evil spell. Your enthusiastic believing will inspire theirs.
- Continually reinforce students' believable acting. Smile and interact with those participating fully. After a dramatization, point out the students who are putting effort and imagination into, for example, becoming a mysterious fog, a hungry dog, or a powerful John Henry.
- Mention and use students' spontaneous gestures. For example, if a student twists and stoops to become a fierce wind, do it too. If someone strokes her hair as a haughty queen, follow her example. This imitation of their actions will inspire confidence, and gestures, and spontaneous actions from them.
- When an acting assignment is evaluated, ask students to focus on which actors "believed the parts they were playing." Ask what specific actions they did to make it seem real.

CONTROL

A good definition of art is giving form and focus to strong feelings and emotions. Teachers legitimately are often concerned that students will get out of control when acting. Control gives drama artistry and purpose. Actors who express powerful emotions that move an audience have learned techniques of artistic control. Exercising artistic control creates self-esteem and is essential to successful, satisfying classroom dramatization.To help instill and maintain control:

- Discuss the need to exercise control to make the drama artistic and worthwhile. Explain how theater and film actors use controlled, stylized actions that have been practiced and often choreographed when they fight, leap, push, or carry out other aggressive actions.
- Use the "freeze" technique to begin and end a dramatization. For example, begin *There Was a Young Lady of Niger,* with the lady "frozen" in the midst of her curtsy. End with a "frozen picture" of her covering her head as if swallowed by the tiger. Have students use the freeze technique when performing informally for the class and on stage.
- Slow down the rate of your speech, and use a low calm voice to slow down students' actions. This technique is helpful when you feel the drama is getting too emotional. Speaking slowly also helps both a speaker and an audience focus on and experience the words, images, and action in the poem.
- Have students act traveling motions "in place." These might include running, climbing hills, prancing, and skipping.
- Model using slow-motion, enlarged movement when doing actions, such as, galloping, floating like a cloud, or galumphing through the woods as the Jabberwocky.
- Do falls in slow motion. For example, when the eagle plummets from his crag, slow down the rate of the action. Say F-A-L-L-S slowly, elongating the word to accommodate a slow drop.
- Use a control device, such as a bell, to begin acting and to end it. For example, say, "When I ring the bell, take the position of the character at the beginning of the poem. When I ring the bell again, freeze in position of the character in the final action of the poem." Have students use a triangle or bell to begin and end the dramatizations that they perform for the class.
- Use peer evaluation to point out times when control was good or to discuss what students might do to exercise more control.
- Encourage students to stand on two feet to play animals, such as the tiger and lamb in William Blake's poems as they can maneuver better and are more visible to the audience.
- End dramatizations with a quiet lyric, such as Carl Sandburg's *Fog* or Emily Dickinson's *Will There Really Be a Morning?*

- Have students illustrate a poem or a favorite line of a poem as a calming finale.

VOICE AND MOVEMENT

Voice and movement mean using different kinds of voices, body movements, and gestures to describe and portray different characters, their actions, and their feelings. These are the basic tools with which actors and reciters portray their parts.

The characters, images, and language in poems are vivid, giving ample opportunity to use expressive voice and movement. For example, Paul Revere gallops energetically to alert the people that the British are coming. The reciter describing Revere's ride must use the same urgency with the voice. In contrast, a star twinkles lightly to brighten the sky, and the reciter must capture the light, magic brightness of starlight with the voice.

To teach voice and movement:

- Have students practice using the voice and movement of two contrasting characters. For example, say, "Go away," as a giant, and then as a tiny mouse. This shows how differing characters with different motivations might say the same words.
- Model by emphasizing using expressive voice and movement.

CHAPTER TWO
The Four Principles of Effective Stage Speech

When you use your voice (and not a microphone), the audience listens to something visceral and energetic. Young people need to learn how to speak poetry.
—Jack O'Brien, artistic director, Old Globe Theatre, San Diego

THE FOUR SPEAKING PRINCIPLES

Poetry more than any other type of writing requires good speaking skills because every word counts. Most poems are short, compact, and full of emotion. Energetic speech and the use of a variety of oral interpretation techniques involves participants and an audience fully in a poem.

Four speaking principles are the foundation of a good speaking program. This chapter describes these four principles and how to teach them. (A detailed description of how to introduce and teach the four principles in a lesson on poetry dramatization is found in Chapter Seven, A Model Lesson.)

This chapter also describes other speaking techniques and gesturing. The best interpreters use a variety of vocal techniques to bring forth all of the nuances of a poem.

The four principles are:

PROJECTION: speaking loudly enough so that every word is heard
ARTICULATION: speaking every consonant in a word distinctly so that the exact word is clear
COLORIZATION: coloring your speech so that words sound like what they describe and adding facial expression and gestures to intensify the meaning
SLOWING THE PACE: slowing the rate of speech to focus on important words and phrases

List the principles on the board and refer to them throughout any lesson.

PROJECTION

Projection means throwing your voice out to the back of a space so that everyone can hear what you're saying. Projection is the first and most important principle. If students project well, other principles likely will follow. It is difficult, for example, to speak rapidly when projecting well.

To instill good projection:

- Have students define projection. Ask what happens to you when you are in an audience and speakers don't project.
- Mention that the most important requirement of an actor is a strong expressive voice. Ask why? Add that when directing a play many directors first look for actors who are able to project their voices.
- Explain that stage acting is the highest form of acting, and that a mike-free projected voice is the most expressive voice.
- Model poor and then good projection. Invite a student to the front of the room and carry on a brief conversation about the weather—first using poor and then good projection. Ask which conversation would be more interesting to an audience and why.
- Practice projection with students—mentioning that it requires using a strong voice and not shouting, which would annoy an audience. Then, have students stand and chant "PROJECTION" four times while throwing an arm outward as if throwing a ball and trying to aim both at the farthest reaches of the room.
- Always reject poor projection. Push for better projection by, if necessary, interrupting and saying "louder." Praise improvement while coaxing students to attain a higher level.
- Emphasize the need for good projection each time students read aloud and always reinforce it when it's accomplished.

ARTICULATION

Articulation means saying every consonant in words distinctly so the exact word is understood. For example, *cat* sounds like "cat" and not "cab" or "can."

Good articulation requires active use of the articulators—teeth, tongue, lips, and gum ridges. The best speakers energetically use their articulators vigorously moving the jaw, lips, and tongue. Good articulation helps participants experience the language fully and sensually on the lips, teeth, tongue, and palate. So, as drama expert Stanley Kauffmann has written, "Even ordinary words can become exciting surprises."

To instill good articulation:

- Model poor and then good articulation. For example, say "dog" swallowing the *g*. Say it again emphasizing the *g*. Ask students to describe the difference in your articulation.
- Ask why poetry that is short demands exceptional articulation.
- Practice using good articulation with them. Have them rise and chant AR-TIC-U-LA-TION four times pointing emphatically at each syllable to dramatize enunciating each syllable clearly.
- Articulate unusual or difficult words from the poems to make sure they pronounce them correctly. For example, try *symmetry, jocund, cauldron, mud-luscious.*
- Recite limericks, particularly tongue-twister limericks such as *The Tutor Who Tooted the Flute* and *A Flea and a Fly in a Flue,* that demand good articulation.
- Model good articulation when reciting poems to students.

COLORIZATION

Colorization means saying words so they sound like what they describe, using facial expression and stylized gestures to illustrate them. For example, say "joy" in a bright, light voice and thrust your arms up exuberantly. Say "gloom" in a dark, deep, low voice while slumping over. Colorization is a distinctive technique of storytellers and actors to help audiences experience the action and imagery.

To develop the technique of colorization:

- Ask students what it means for speakers to speak colorfully when reciting poetry. Make a big colorful gesture as you say "colorfully" and use a colorful voice.

- Have students rise and chant "colorization" four times, each time opening their arms out in big, wide, colorful gestures and opening their eyes as if enlivened.
- Recite a Mother Goose rhyme focusing on using colorful speech. For example, say "Humpty Dumpty" in a big, full voice. Recite "Sat on a wall," heavily. Vocally stretch out the word "F-A-L-L" as he plummets off a high wall. Increase the rate of speech to simulate the prancing horsemen in "All the king's horses, and all the king's men." Slow down your speech and shrug hopelessly on "Couldn't put Humpty together again."
- Let student choose rhymes to recite line by line, making each word as colorful as possible.

SLOWING THE PACE

It requires discipline in our speeded-up society to slow the pace. Drama and the recitation of poetry or any literature should never be rushed. Slowing the rate of speech helps participants and the audience concentrate on and enjoy every important word and line of a poem.

Although some scenes and lines of poetry call for a quickening pace, normally it is best to slow the pace so that the actors and audience can enjoy and understand the poem.

Speakers are often struck at how attentively audiences respond when they consciously slow down the rate of speech and create big, slow gestures.

To instill slowing the pace:

- Model a slow rate of speech and action yourself. For example, when introducing a lesson, slow the rate of your motions as you hold a triangle high; strike it three times, taking time to turn and face the left, right, and center of the room; make a leisurely, large, welcoming gesture with your arms, and freeze demonstrating slow, artistic control.
- Ask students why it's important to recite poetry slowly.
- Model a too-speedy delivery of a Mother Goose rhyme or a limerick and then a slowed-down version. Ask students which an audience would prefer and why.
- Have students stand and chant with you "SLOW THE PACE," four times, slowly opening your arms out to your sides and pausing after each word—SLOW, THE, and PACE—to emphasize speaking and gesturing slowly.

- Enlarge and slow down all of your gestures and your recitation when you model reciting any poem.
- Let students choose a Mother Goose rhyme, such as *Twinkle, Twinkle Little Star* or a simple song such as "Row, Row, Row, Your Boat" to sing focusing on slowing the pace. Perhaps recite and dramatize it as if making a film in slow motion.

GESTURING

The action of a gesture creates the feeling of the language. Gesturing is a form of colorization and helps enliven speech. Gestures help you remember and experience the language because the words become visceral. Gestures also promote projection, and they help English language learners understand the words.

The teacher should model gesturing slowly. Slow stylized gestures help you fully experience the feeling of the language and can be beautiful like a dance. A group of students gesturing simultaneously indeed looks like a choreographed dance.

Facial expression further vitalizes the gesture. For example, a disgruntled person might scowl, a fierce tiger bare his teeth, or a surprised person open her eyes and mouth wide and raise her eyebrows. Gesture suggestions are given with each line in most poems in this book.

Other Speaking Techniques:

EMPHASIS: stress on important words through variation in volume, pitch, pause, gesture, and facial expression

INFLECTION: vocal technique in which the voice rises or falls. Rising inflection carries thoughts and ideas forward. A falling inflection indicates the end of a thought or idea.

PAUSE: stopping after a word or phrase. Most beginners don't hold a pause long enough.

PITCH: how low or high your voice is. Usually recite poetry in normal range and extend the range when the character, mood, or intensity of the scene require it.

RATE: how fast or slow you speak. In scenes of excitement or quickening hoofbeats, quicken the pace. In death scenes or dreamy states, slow it down. Changing the rate at appropriate points is dramatic.

VOCAL QUALITY: whether the voice is shrill, raspy, lilting, simpering, barking, booming

VOCALIZED SOUND EFFECTS AND SINGING: adding barks, growls, whimpers, yelps, cries. You might even sing lines or stanzas. Vocalizations and singing can heighten the emotional and dramatic effect, but they must be used with discretion.

VOLUME: loudness or softness of voice. For a soft voice, use a stage whisper that communicates to an audience.

Developing the Speaking Techniques:

- Dramatize short poems or stanzas as ten-minute fillers. Frequent dramatization builds skills and involvement quickly.
- Focus on one or two of the fundamentals each time the students recite—PROJECTION, ARTICULATION, COLORIZATION, OR SLOWING THE PACE. The poems in this book have students do this.
- Have students underline important words to stress and make slash marks in places to pause. Then, recite a poem implementing these techniques.
- Have students create gestures for each line of a poem and recite the poem using them.
- Practice lifting the ends of lines with no punctuation.
- Insist on good posture—feet planted firmly with no swaying, fidgeting, hands in the pocket, or other nervous mannerisms.

CHAPTER THREE

The Mechanics

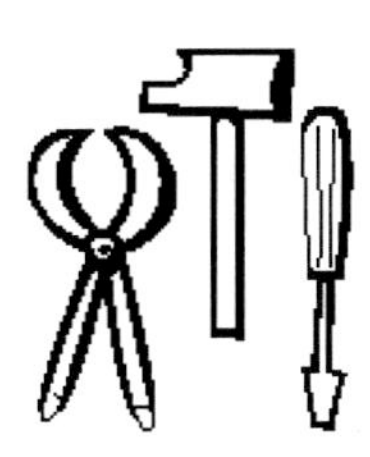

Poetry lasts because it gives the ever-changing pleasures of being both a statement and a song.
—Paul Valery

This chapter contains tips on how to set up the classroom and teach poetry dramatization to inspire the most involvement from students.

USING VISUAL AIDES

The right photo, painting, or other visual aid helps students understand the subject or concept of a poem. Pictures of the Euphrates, Nile, and Mississippi Rivers could illustrate *The Negro Speaks of Rivers;* while the figure of the Greek god Pan, alluded to in e. e. cummings poem *In Just-* would help the reader. Visuals, of course, are particularly valuable to help English-language learners understand and enter the poem.

Even familiar subjects such as an eagle or a robin can be heightened by finding pictures, photos, or films of these birds. Perhaps, bring in an object mentioned in the poem, such as a metal pail for Shakespeare's *Winter* or a bunch of daffodils to introduce *I Wandered Lonely as a Cloud*. Films of historic Boston and the events leading to the American Revolution could add depth to an interpretation of *Paul Revere's Ride*

The books, *Talking to the Sun* and *Imaginary Gardens* (listed in the Bibliography), include photos and illustrations of some authors and poems in this book. *Paul Revere's Ride, The Ballad of John Henry*, and *Annabel Lee* have been illustrated in picture books. Other sources of visual aids are wildlife calendars and pictorial history books.

WAYS OF DRAMATIZING

The following suggests ways to dramatize poems from the most basic of recitation and gesturing to the most complex methods of staging poems as plays with costumes and instruments.

ECHOING: The teacher or leader recites each line, and the students recite it after him.

CHORAL DRAMATIZING: The teacher recites and dramatizes every line while the group recites and dramatizes with the leader.

SYNCHRONIZED GESTURING: One member of a small group recites the poem while the group does a gesture for each line. In groups of four, each person might take a turn saying a line while the other three dramatize it. Synchronized gesturing looks like choreographed dancing and is fascinating to watch and to do.

CREATING A POETRY RADIO SHOW: Individuals recite, or pairs alternate reciting, lines of the poem using only their voices and, possibly, rhythm instruments.

DRAMATIZING INDIVIDUAL LINES: A poem is scripted as a play assigning each line of the poem to a character or object that the line describes. Shakespeare's *Winter* is scripted this way. For example, the Icicles recite and act the first line as follows: "When icicles hang by the wall." The owl recites and acts this line as follows: "When nightly stares the owl."

DRAMATIZING STANZAS FROM CLASSICS: The teacher assigns small groups one or two stanzas from longer classics, such as *The Rime of the Ancient Mariner, The Highway Man,* or *The Odyssey.* Students focus on practicing articulation and creating actions to go with each line. Groups perform their dramatizations for the class. These short dramatizations may stimulate interest in reading and dramatizing the whole poem.

PERFORMING INFORMALLY: With only their classmates as audience, pairs or small groups of students recite a poem and act the characters and objects. A sound crew plays instruments to accentuate the action, and costume pieces are added. Poems in this book are scripted to be dramatized in this way.

PERFORMING AS TRAVELING TROUPES OR IN ASSEMBLIES: Outstanding groups of students dramatize one or more poems in other classrooms or present one or more poems as part of a patriotic, holiday, or other assembly. A sound crew may play instruments, and costume pieces may be added.

RECITING MEMORIZED POEMS: Individuals recite a short class-memorized poem.

CHOOSING, MEMORIZING, AND COSTUMING A POEM: Individuals or small groups choose a poem from their texts or other sources and do a polished dramatization for the class. This might be in place of, or part of, a poetry report or project.

STAGING A POETRY PERFORMANCE: Students or the teacher decide which poems to dramatize in a recital for a large audience. Choose one or several of the ways listed above or use other methods, or stage the Poetry Performance Script in this book.

CREATING A THEATER IN YOUR CLASSROOM

TRADITIONAL STAGING

The classroom makes a good traditional stage. Designate areas on each side of the stage as "offstage" where actors wait to enter to play their roles. Place the sound crew along one side of the room so that they are visible to the audience and can see the actors to coordinate their effects with the actions of the actors. The reciter stands on the opposite side of the room as the sound crew.

THEATRE IN THE ROUND

An interesting way to dramatize poetry is to stage it in a circle with both the audience and the actors sitting around the staging area. A circle creates an intimate atmosphere and invites participation. Actors step into the center to act their roles and sit down when their roles are finished.

Circle dramatization allows fluidity of movement. Actors can appear and disappear quickly. It's a challenge to devise ways to perform in a circle so that everyone sees the important action. Some poems in this book that work well dramatized in a circle are *In Just-, Fog,* and *I Wandered Lonely as a Cloud.*

AREA STAGING

Some story poems or ballads benefit from being staged in different areas in the room. The different areas might represent various places the character travels to. For example, Richard Cory, who strolls downtown, might stroll up and down the aisles. In *Paul Revere's Ride,* the front of the room might be Boston, the center the river, and the back the area where he makes his ride. Area staging is visually interesting and allows freer movement as the actors can move about.

ORGANIZING SMALL GROUPS

Students are often the most involved when they direct and stage a dramatization themselves. Assign small-group dramatizations twice a week for a month or so, and students will feel comfortable with drama and have the skills to create ingenious dramatizations on their own.

Pairs or groups of four are the most effective. To help students get immediately on task, assign roles for groups by numbering the script and assigning each student a number.

Give students one or two goals, such as speaking so that all can understand and doing an action to go with each line. Allow 15 minutes or less to practice. A short rehearsal focuses creativity. Begin with short, active, humorous poems. Limericks make a good beginning, small-group lesson.

STUDENT REFLECTION

Students benefit from reflecting on their experience of dramatization. Ask:

What did you enjoy doing most?
How did you feel playing your role or an instrument?
What was most difficult to do?
What role would you like to play next time?
What would you like to add to your dramatization?
What other poems would you like to dramatize?

STUDENT EVALUATION

Evaluation is essential to help students develop drama and theatre skills. To improve the drama, comments must be specific describing precisely what was done with the voice or body to make the drama effective. Thus, saying she was "a good eagle" is vague. More helpful comments would be that the actor made her hands like claws clasping the crag, that she spread her arms like hovering wings and thrust her body forward as if plummeting into the sea. The specific comments let the actors know exactly what they did to make their parts believable and the comments help other students learn the kinds of actions needed to play a role.

To promote specific comments ask:

What did the actors do with their movements to create a majestic eagle, a blazing sun, a rippling sea, or the crag?
What did the reciters do with their voices to make the words clear and exciting? What speaking skills were used well?
How were the sound effects played to enhance the action and help the actors act their roles?
What might be done next time to add to the performance? For example, what might the eagle do to show that he is peering for fish? What might the sun do to show her brightness? In what other ways might the crag be formed?

ADVANCED STUDENT EVALUATION

More advanced drama students might use this checklist to evaluate their own dramatizations:

Am I projecting my voice?
Am I keeping my body open so that I'm sharing the meaning with the audience?
Am I making the meaning of the poem clear?
Am I using a variety of vocal techniques?
Are my movements clear and appropriate to the action of the poem? Do my movements enhance the meaning of the words?
Is my staging interesting?

MEMORIZATION

Memorizing a poem creates a feeling of power and comfort. Other benefits of memorization are:

- Memorizing a poem shows that the poem is valuable to you.
- Reciters of memorized poems experience the poem fully and share the experience directly and fully with an audience.
- Poems memorized as a youngster tend to stay with you.

- Learning poems teaches you to focus on a single task and creates a feeling of mastery and confidence.
- Language learners learn the best usage of English and experience the cadence of the English language

WAYS TO MEMORIZE

Begin with rhyming couplets, Mother Goose rhymes, and other short rhyming poems.

To memorize longer poems, one teacher had students learn a four-line stanza each day. He wrote the poem on big paper and hung it on the door so that the students saw it when they lined up or left the room. By the end of the week, students knew the poem. He put the memorized poetry in loose-leaf notebooks and placed them around the room. Twice a year he had poetry recitals in which students recited poems they'd memorized.

A helpful way to memorize is to copy the poem by hand. This gives the students kinesthetic input. They become aware of each word, the layout of the words on the page, and even the punctuation.

CHAPTER FOUR
Directing a Poetry Performance

Talk little. Do much.
—Francis Hodge, director-author.

The poetry performance in this book can be produced in two weeks. Schedule daily rehearsals of about an hour for up to thirty-five students. No drama experience is necessary. The script takes about twenty-five minutes to perform, and everyone plays a significant role.

The script can be copied from this book and distributed to each performer. During the performance, only the storytellers and the sound crew need scripts. The dramatized poems in this book use the narrative mime approach to dramatization.

In narrative mime theatre, four storytellers position themselves on the stage (two on each side) and use scripts to introduce and recite poems. The actors, dressed in black, sit in a semicircle on stage. Their simple costume pieces, props, and fabrics (to create scenery) are under their chairs.

When a storyteller recites a poem, the actors have their props ready and step forward onto the stage to act their parts. For example, when a storyteller recites "An epicure dining at Crewe...," the epicure actor wearing a top hat stands and walks snootily onto the stage. Costume suggestions for all the poems are at the end of the script.

A sound crew of six, dressed in black, sit at one or two long tables at the side of the stage with rhythm or homemade instruments to create sound effects. The crew might also use a piano to make some effects. (Piano players need not know how to play the piano.) The table and piano are placed so that the crew can see the actors and the audience can watch the crew and see the effects being made. (See diagram.) All of the sound cues are in the script.

This book contains a complete performance script with poems of different types including nonsense verse, limericks, nature and animal poems, and a patriotic song or poem finale. Students or teachers might also create their own script based on a subject or theme using poems from this book or others. (For ideas on creating your own script, see Chapter 8, Choosing and Adapting Poems to Dramatize.)

This chapter describes techniques that may be used to cast, direct, and produce the script with students of varying academic and English-language abilities. It also outlines ways to train the audience in basic theatre techniques to provide feedback for the performers and the director. This involvement deepens the audience's understanding of and appreciation for theater-performance skills and may inspire some to want to perform too.

THE STYLE OF POETRY PERFORMANCE

The characters and objects in poetry dramatization are universal forces or types—the haughty duchess, the lyrical moon, the mysterious fog, the majestic eagle, and the tricky fox.

Actors' movements must be stylized and enlarged so the audience can immediately identify the type. Each must have its own distinctive movement style.

The style of a poetry performance is *presentational*, meaning the performers present the material directly to the audience. It differs from *realism*, in which actors frequently turn and talk to other characters pretending they are in their own world and the audience doesn't exist.

In presentational theatre, actors open up their bodies and share their movements, expressions, and thoughts with the audience, frequently pantomiming actions and exaggerating facial expressions. Blocking techniques to achieve this interaction are in the script.

THEATER OF THE IMAGINATION

Poetry dramatization emphasizes the development of the imagination. Visual and audio interpretation of characters and objects are presented as they are described by the storytellers or other actors. Filmy blue fabric held by two actors across the back of the stage represents "spacious skies." Wiggling hands create twinkling stars. Actors with orange baseball caps gnaw bones and become greedy little foxes.

Sound effects are executed in full view, serving to emphasize the language and the action. This type of presentation demands that both the actors and the audience use their imaginations to fill in the details and bring the characters and action to life.

LEARNING HOW TO DIRECT

Even experienced directors look for ways to enrich their directing by learning new techniques. Directors and artists of all types borrow and get ideas everywhere. Indeed, the most experienced directors can get fresh ideas watching, for example, street theatre.

Three ways to learn to direct are to act and direct yourself, to attend school, community, and professional productions of all types, and to read directing and acting books.

Many directors have acted and have learned through experience what kinds of directions inspired them and helped them act. This kind of experience helps you know what to say and do when trying to help your students act.

When directing yourself, you quickly learn what works with your actors and staging and what doesn't. Practical solutions must be found. For example, if a reciter isn't projecting, you must find a way to help her project, or some other solution. When the action on stage is overcrowded or if sound crew members aren't playing their effects on cue, you must find solutions to these problems.

A good way to learn to direct is to attend school, amateur, and professional productions. Observing amateur productions is valuable because you learn by seeing strengths and flaws. Sometimes these directors have ingenious ideas for movement, staging, costume pieces, and scenery that work well with amateurs and on limited budgets. You also see what to avoid and what must be strong in your directing. For example, clear voice and movement style and strong entrances and exits are essentials.

Acting and directing books can be inspirational and help directors improve their skills. (Some good ones are listed in the Bibliography.) Good books help you focus on the essentials and give you a big picture of the art of directing that can enrich your production.

THE DIRECTOR'S ROLES

THE DIRECTOR AS LEADER

The director's first job is to "direct" and lead people: A director must be very organized and know what the goals are for each rehearsal. To forge a creative bond, it helps to communicate the goals and the procedure that will be followed to achieve them at the beginning of each rehearsal. Everyone feels a sense of security and purpose if they know what they are aiming for. Organization also saves time.

For example, at a first rehearsal, explain how the production will be done, display the costumes, set the chairs in a semicircle on the stage and the tables for the sound crew next to the stage area with instruments on them. At the beginning of the rehearsal, tell students how the performance will be produced by explaining how the costumes and instruments will be used. Then, tell them which scenes you'll be rehearsing that day.

THE DIRECTOR AS INSPIRER AND CONFIDENCE-BUILDER

Beginning artists learn by imitating. Thus, the director should continually model the enthusiastic behavior desired. For example, always use an expressive, projected voice and clear movements.

If students don't understand your directions, act the role yourself, doing an exaggerated demonstration of it. For example, to help them act a hungry dog, leap onto the stage, crouch, hold up your paws, and pant eagerly. Your enjoyment of playing will transfer to them, creating confidence and a willingness to jump in and play the part.

Everyone needs praise. Beginning performers need a lot of encouragement to reinforce their efforts. It takes courage to go before an audience. Some students understandably feel vulnerable when they expose their imaginations and themselves in such direct, physical ways. The experience is a new one, and the creative process is delicate. Support, encouragement, and appreciation will help beginning artists develop their talents and gain self-confidence so that they will hunger to do more.

It is most beneficial to begin every rehearsal by mentioning what students have done well. Focus on anything that is contributing to the endeavor. Compliment students on how well they are working as a team, how attentive and focused they are, how much they've learned and accomplished quickly, and how impressed you are by their use of imagination and their enthusiasm for theatre.

This general reinforcement will go a long way toward making students feel as though they comprise a successful, creative team. It builds confidence. They become committed to the production, and they love to play more and more.

An effective way to get students involved and to heighten and improve the playing is to ask them what they think was done effectively and what else might be done to improve the production. Encouraging them to articulate their thoughts on the production shows them that you appreciate their insights, teaches them how to observe and articulate what makes a good performance, and forges a creative bond between the performers and director.

Also and perhaps most importantly, students tend to be eager and willing to push for improvements that are their own ideas. Students often listen to each others' ideas with more enthusiasm and interest than to ideas expressed by the director.

THE DIRECTOR AS COACH

While reinforcing students, the director must also act like an athletic coach pushing students to improve. This direct exhortation is essential in getting students to fulfill such technical requirements as speaking with projection, creating clear enlarged gestures, speaking slowly, and using enthusiasm throughout rehearsals.

Of course, good projection is essential. If reciters don't project, the director should interrupt immediately and say "PROJECT." Coaching them to project will have to be continual because it isn't a habit, but this coaching pays off with an alive and audible performance.

Performers respond well to an assertive director just as athletes do to a coach who buoys them up and pushes them to achieve their best. This approach should, of course, be coupled with hearty praise for improvement and effort.

THE DIRECTOR AS ARTISTIC COLLABORATOR

Theatre is a collaborative art. The director depends on the actors' involvement and input to put on an effective production. Indeed, perhaps the most productive and fulfilling aspect of directing a student play is to reinforce, encourage, and use students' input whenever possible. Students become excited and committed to a production when their ideas are highlighted, honored, and used. It fosters a feeling of creative empowerment, opens up their imaginations, and gives students confidence to risk offering more ideas.

Students' fresh ideas also inspire the production and give the director ideas for this and future productions. For example, a director of Poe's *The Raven* felt a raven outfit might appear comic and detract from the poem. A student suggested the actor wear a black cape creating a symbolic raven, which worked very well.

Naturally the director has the final say on what to include—but not all ideas are feasible or beneficial. If an idea cannot be used, show appreciation for the contribution and explain why it is not right for this production. For example, if someone suggests wearing full costumes, explain that theatre of the imagination focuses on acting and the use of the imagination and not on elaborate costumes.

FINDING CREATIVE SOLUTIONS TO PERFORMANCE PROBLEMS

Directors can become frustrated if performers do not do what the part requires. It is tempting to hammer away at the actor to get him to "do it right," but this can be counterproductive for everyone concerned. Indeed, performances do not improve under tense pressure, as both the director and students may lose enthusiasm for the project.

Creative solutions can be found for acting or performance problems. If a performer is not doing what you request after several tries, it is usually best just to skip it and continue with the rehearsal. A solution may be found later, or the problem may resolve itself. The student may not really want to play the part, a possibility that can be discussed later. If an actor cannot speak loudly enough, for example, you might have another student speak the line with him.

AVOIDING THE BURDEN OF PERFECTIONISM

Many directors of beginners feel hassled, especially as the performance time nears. The production method for these poems is designed to avoid much of the harried director syndrome by having limited line memorization and by including so much action as well as visual and auditory stimulation that if one thing does not work perfectly or is off cue, something else immediately makes up for it.

A way to avoid the burden of perfectionism is to keep your primary goal in mind at all times. If the goal for these students is that they first and foremost enjoy the experience so that they will want to do more, the burden of perfectionism can be lifted.

Perfection is not possible nor even desired. Perfection can be stultifying, hindering spontaneity and the creative process. Instead, give students two goals. First, tell them to focus on playing their roles fully. For example, if playing a frightened mouse, they should make themselves look small and skitter to hide from enemies; if playing a storyteller, they must speak in a way to excite the audience; if a sound crew member, they must be on cue and play instruments crisply to communicate to the audience. Second, remind students to work as a team, being ready to help each other when problems arise. Giving students these two clear goals helps reduce self-consciousness and stage fright by giving them things to do to focus their attention.

STAGE ACTING TECHNIQUES

Several acting techniques will enhance the quality of your production.

CHOOSING A CHARACTER OR NEUTRAL STANCE

Each character needs a stance that communicates clearly to the audience who that character is and what she is doing. For example, hungry Mr. Fox might crouch alertly with paws and nose up ready to pounce on prey. The majestic eagle might raise arms to resemble wings ready to plunge into the sea.

Students should assume their character stance or a neutral stance whenever they are not in the action. A neutral stance is standing still in a dignified posture with no swaying, hands in pockets, fidgeting, or other distractions. Storytellers and other reciters always stand in neutral when not dramatizing a line.

MIMING

Narrative mime theatre uses few props, and the audience depends on actors to pretend that specific objects exist and are being manipulated. To mime successfully, actors must envision that the object is there and that they are using it for a purpose. For example, the greedy old person from Leeds must visualize the size and feeling of the packet of seeds that he wants to eat. He must rip it open to relieve his hunger, pull out seeds, and chew them ravenously.

To mime for the stage, essential details are exaggerated, slowed down and emphasized so that they are clearly communicated and the feeling behind the gesture is heightened. For example, Mrs. Slipper Slopper opens her eyes wide, thrusts her head emphatically forward, and cups her mouth with her hands as she calls for help from her husband.

PLAYING SCENERY AND INANIMATE OBJECTS

Playing scenery and inanimate objects develops the imagination. Scenery can be acted in pairs or small groups giving shy students nonthreatening yet stimulating roles. Indeed, it's always possible to add one more tree, rock, or daffodil to give more students opportunities to play roles.

The following tips will help students play objects:

- Students should have props or fabrics ready to use so they can create the object instantaneously.

- Students should portray the object's quality. For example, to create falling snow, students must manipulate long white ribbons on dowels with flowing motions to create the flying flakes.
- Students should act only when storytellers cue them. For example, Paul Revere gallops "in place" to each destination as the narration describes it and then freezes when he arrives at the spot. He resumes galloping again only when the narration continues the journey—again stopping when that segment is spoken and done.
- Students should sit or freeze when their action is over waiting for their next cue.

MOTIVATION

Drama is action. Understanding why a character behaves in a certain way helps actors to act. Actions are done for a reason. For example, Paul Revere tells his friend that the British are coming to alert the people of the invasion. The man in *Windy Nights* gallops nightly on horseback to find relief from his pain. The Moon sheds her beams to "silver" everything below with night's mystery.

Understanding a character's motivation helps actors remember their blocking and do their actions with conviction. Motivations are not in the script. But any time a director can find (or even make up) a reason for what a character is doing, it will help the actors play their parts with purpose and conviction. Give the motivation as an active verb: A character may want to seize power, to find love, or to create beauty. The more urgent the action or motivation the better. For example, tell the greedy person from Leeds to eat the seeds as if he hadn't eaten for a month.

Reciters and the sound crew have reasons for what they do too. A reciter's motivation is to help the audience understand and enjoy the poem. The sound crew's motivation is to create effects to help the audience fully experience the language and to help the actors do their actions.

PUTTING YOURSELF IN THE SHOES, FUR, OR FEATHERS OF A CHARACTER—THE "MAGIC IF"

The great Russian director Stanislavski created and developed an acting method called the "magic if." An actor considers "what if" I were in this character's circumstance, what would I do? The more students can make believe the more authentic their acting will be. The director can help by creating a vivid picture of the character and the situation.

For example, a student becoming a lion would try to imagine he is covered with a thick coat of golden fur, that he walks on padded paws and has strong, powerful legs and shoulders with which he can pounce forcefully on prey. Actors becoming stormy winds can experience their bodies as mighty winds desiring to make ships and trees toss and sway in their power. (For more information on Believing and other acting techniques, see Chapter one, The Three Principles of Good Acting.)

TRAINING THE SOUND CREW

Audiences frequently say a highlight of a poetry dramatization show is the sound effects. Making sound effects heightens the musicality of the language and punctuates the action. Creating sound effects also helps students develop musical intelligence.

To create effective sound effects:

- Come in on cue. The crew should highlight their parts, follow their scripts carefully, and get instruments ready ahead of time.
- Create the quality of the sound imitated. For example, punctuate the punch line in a limerick, by shaking a tambourine vigorously and slapping it in the center. To simulate a man on a galloping horse, strike a wood block rhythmically and briskly. Some students instinctively create precise sound qualities. Others need modeling
- Capture the theatrical clarity and brightness of the effects by playing them crisply and emphatically. Limp effects don't communicate. For example, strike a triangle sharply for falling rain. Ring jingle bells brightly for a "cat in a flurry."
- Make sure that the crew can see the action on stage to coordinate sound effects with the actors' actions. The effects also help the actors to act.

INCORPORATING MUSIC

A musical overture to a performance sets the tone and helps the audience and the performers get ready for the performance. The performance script suggests using Mozart's *Eine Kleine Nacht Musik* or a section from Vivaldi's *The Four Seasons* to set a happy bright classic mood.

Other selections might be used to introduce different sections of poems, such as Rossini's *The Thieving Magpie Pie t*o begin nonsense verse, *Pineapple Rag* by Scott Joplin to introduce limericks, selections from *Carnival of the Animals* to begin the animal poems, and Debussy's *La Mer* or *Claire de Lune* or Stravinsky's *Rite of Spring* for the nature section.

CASTING

Many agree a good script and thoughtful casting are the most important elements of a successful production. For example, a confident, animated Storyteller will begin a performance with vitality and good projection, setting the tone and inspiring other performers. Minimal line memorization greatly enhances the possibility of getting the right student in the right part.

Three methods of casting a play are given below. Using more than one method is a good idea so that you can see students in different situations and gauge their ability and commitment. Regardless of what method is used, keep the casting flexible, so that students' parts may be changed. Having the right student in the right part enhances the production and inspires the performance of the other students.

The Preliminary Tryout

For a preliminary tryout, have students act some of the poems in this book in pairs and groups informally and then present them to the class. You will see who has the most natural acting ability, who has the best voice, and who is most interested. Those who perform limply or with little confidence may need to build confidence by first playing smaller parts.

The Written Tryout

A written tryout helps students articulate what the role requires and shows their commitment to the production.

For the written tryout, follow the steps below:

- Have students list three roles they want to play in order of preference (roles include acting, storytelling, and sound crew).
- Have students describe what the characters are like or, in the case of storytellers or sound crew, what is required to play the role effectively.
- Have students explain why they should be chosen to play the role and what they would try to do to play their part well.

Evaluate these responses and make your choices.

The Formal Tryout
For the formal tryout, you choose parts of the script for students to recite and act. They go to the front of the room or stage to try out for the roles they want. It's best to try out in the space where you'll perform as projection and movement ability are more obvious. The formal tryout allows you to focus on each individual, perhaps giving some directions and pointers to see how students respond and compare with each other. Rate reciters on vocal projection and gesturing and on the ability to take directions.

SPOTTING THE BORN ACTOR

The most important quality of a good actor is a strong expressive voice. This is essential for reciting poetry that is short and in which every word counts. The more speaking and movement skills the actor-reciter has the more fully the poem will come alive for an audience.

There is such a thing as a born actor. The born actor is able to jump inside and express the feelings of many characters. Born actors are also hungry to act and will do so at any opportunity. The best of them will listen eagerly to and even solicit the director's ideas, then try to follow them wholeheartedly because they are very involved with the part and anxious to act it well.

Born actors also come up with many ideas for parts and do them spontaneously during rehearsals. They contribute to the direction of the play through their enthusiasm, intuition, imagination, and natural skills. These students have strong voices and expressive bodies with good kinesthetic skills. They are comfortable on stage and love to play. Not all born actors will have all of these traits in equal degree, but they will have most of them.

For a performance to please an audience, it is often helpful to put the most competent actors in leading roles. Some might argue that leading roles should be spread out democratically, and for classroom dramatization this is a good idea. When performing before an audience, however, the students, audience and director will feel more comfortable if a strong actor who is able and eager to handle the part is in the biggest role.

The strong actor will inspire the students and director. The actor's confidence and spontaneous acting ideas will put more timid students at ease. Encourage these strong actors to work with other students acting some poems with them to help give them confidence and create an atmosphere of teamwork.

Occasionally two or three students are equally good actors. If in doubt, choose the most responsible student with the strongest voice for the most important role. In leading roles particularly, it is essential an actor be heard. A student who is reliable, follows directions, and gives 100 percent effort will improve over time.

If all contenders fit these criteria, then you will have to choose one. Mention that every excellent actor has had the experience of not getting a desired role. Indeed, success is due to hard work, willingness to play a less-desired role for the experience, and persistence despite adversity.

BLOCKING

One of the director's most important functions is to give actors their blocking. Good blocking enables the audience to see what is going on and focuses attention on the important action of the moment. Good blocking has flow and a variety of movement. It combines movement and frozen pictures or still shots.

To help describe the blocking to actors, the stage is divided into areas. (See diagram.) Some areas get more attention than others. For example, standing center stage naturally gets more attention than standing upstage left. Downstage areas are often strong because they are close to the audience. Characters usually talk to the audience from downstage.

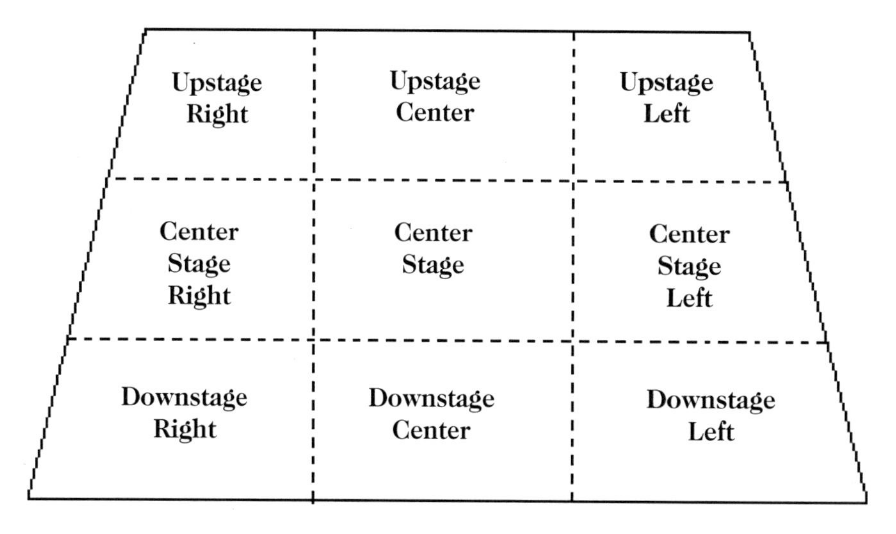

The term *upstage* dates back to a time when stages were *raked* or sloped upward. The area opposite upstage is downstage. Stage right and left are identified from the actors' point of view. As mentioned, some areas are stronger than others, though it is best to use every stage area, even the corners, to open up the stage's full potential and to keep the action from looking confined or cluttered.

To help students learn the areas, draw the diagram on the board, discuss it, and have students practice moving to the various areas in front of the classroom. One way to do this is to use Mother Goose verse. First choose two students to play Jack and Jill; tell them they will go to different stage areas on each line. Have them begin by standing downstage center. Tell them on "Jack and Jill went up the hill," to go upstage; on "To fetch a pail of water," say to go upstage left. Tell Jack on "Jack fell down and broke his crown," to go center stage left. Tell Jill on "Jill came tumbling after," to go downstage center. The term *stage* might not be used when giving the directions, and you might just say, "Go up right" or "Move down left."

There are four blocking techniques students must use to share a performance with an audience:

- Open up to the audience.
- Don't let another actor stand in front of you or crowd you.
- Use all of the stage.
- Maintain stillness when you are not acting, with no fidgeting.

To practice these techniques, invite a student to the front of the room, and you recite *Little Miss Muffet*, facing the student in profile. Then, recite it again, this time opening up your body in a three-quarter position, so that most of your face and body is visible to the students sitting in the center. Ask which position is better to share the rhyme with the audience.

Mention and show how the open position must be adjusted to open up the action to all three sides of the audience and not just the center. You might compare body position during a conversation in life to that used during a dialogue or mime interaction in the theatre.

Ask another student to the front of the room. This time, stand in front of the student while you recite the rhyme. Ask what actors might do if they find themselves in this situation on stage. An obvious answer is to step aside so that you will be seen by the audience. Another is to step back so that the other actor must also step back in order to talk to you.

Ask a third student to the front and ask them to recite *Little Miss Muffet*, while you fidget and shift your feet back and forth. Ask what you did that would distract an audience. Ask what you might do instead to keep the audience's focus on the speaker. The obvious answer is to stand still, keeping hands quiet, and looking at the other actor to get the audience to focus there.

CHECK THE SIGHT LINES

Sometimes at performances, directors go to a side of the auditorium and realize that the audience cannot see what is going on from that viewpoint. To prevent this from happening, view the whole performance from all parts of the audience or have an assistant do this during rehearsals.

FOCUS ON THE IMPORTANT ACTION

Blocking must focus the audience's attention on the most important action occurring on the stage at the moment. An entering character or reciter should be a focus. So, entrances and exits of reciters or characters must be strong. A good character entrance establishes immediately who the character is and tells the audience exactly what the character is doing.

Use the following guidelines and techniques to help focus attention.

- Place important characters or objects in prominent positions such as center stage or down right.
- Create strong character entrances and exits by having them use clear gestures and movement, going into the center stage or to another strong area when they enter the stage.
- Create frozen pictures to accentuate important images moments and actions.
- Have characters turn (perhaps with backs to the audience), look at a new entering character, freeze and gesture toward the character.
- Focus on the new character by looking directly at them.
- Have characters turn their bodies directly toward the speaking or prominent actor. Emphasize this by pointing with arms, legs, torso, or all three.
- Maintain stillness. No fidgeting, hands in pocket, or other distractions that will shift the focus of attention.

CREATE SPECTACLE, VARIETY, AND DRAMATIC INTEREST

Blocking should be varied and have dramatic interest. The vivid and unusual imagery of poetry is heightened through the use of visual variety.

- Use the full stage (including the extremes from far upstage to far downstage). The spectacle and dramatic power of full stage use can be great. This is necessary in crowd scenes and when many are moving at once.

Spectacle scenes or scenes of pageantry such as the displaying of all of the images in *America the Beautiful* are heightened by using all stage areas. Students on their own will not usually use the extremes of the stage, so just send them there. They tend to cluster together, perhaps due to nervousness.

- "Spike the set," placing white or glow-in-the-dark tape in the spots where you want actors to go.
- Place students at different levels by having some lie down, some sit, some kneel on one or both knees, some stand bent over, some erect with hands up, and so on. Use sturdy chairs or boxes to create various elevations.
- Place inanimate objects on different levels to create varied stage pictures. For example, in Tennyson's *The Eagle,* the sea actors might sit rippling the cloth; the crag might kneel; the sun might stand on a chair; and the sky might be on another chair with the actor reaching above the sun.
- Have actors move on different levels—high, middle, and low. For example, a moon might tiptoe silvering the world with beams. Monkeys can leap high. Lions crouch and paw in middle level and mice skitter close to the ground. Different types of movement also lend variety

STAGING VARIATIONS

Another way to create variety is to vary the way the poems are performed. Try some of the following variations:

- Begin a poem with all of the reciters' backs to the audience and have each turn and face the audience when reciting.
- Use the "line-around method" in which each member of a large group recites one line.
- Perform the poems in pairs, trios, fours, and so on.
- Have the girls and boys recite alternating lines, couplets, or stanzas.
- Have two students go back and forth reciting alternating lines of a poem while the group dramatizes the lines as they recite.
- Recite and then sing ballads or poetic songs. This is done with "America the Beautiful" in the performance script and it might be done with *The Ballad of Mr. Fox.*
- Make a simple backdrop using fish netting on the back of the stage and attaching cutouts of stars, shells, flowers, leaves, or other motifs suitable to your production.

THE PROFESSIONAL CURTAIN CALL

The curtain call ends the show and is the last impression the audience has of the performance. It should be professional and have panache. A well-staged curtain call makes students feel professional and can influence their attitude toward the performance. The techniques of presenting oneself in a curtain call can transfer to other public situations in which a confident, professional stance is required. We all need an effective public persona at times in order to be a success.

In the Poetry Performance Script in this book four storyteller-leaders lead the curtain call. Have the storytellers conduct the proceedings by announcing each group of performers individually. Begin with the actors, then identify the sound crew, and finally the storytellers.

When each group of performers is called, they stand and in turn step forward, saying their names loudly and clearly. When they all have spoken, they step center stage, face the performers, and lift their hands in the air. All performers do this, and when the storytellers' hands are lowered and they bow, the performers do the same and then sit quietly.

A frequent flaw is that students says their names too softly. Insist that they project and say their names loudly, like a cheer. This may need continual work with some, but it is worth the effort indoctrinating them in an important public speaking skill and building confidence and esteem. Point out that they deserve to cheer their names because they have done an excellent job. Practice the curtain call several times, explaining its importance in ensuring that the performance concludes with energy and style.

INVOLVING THE AUDIENCE

A pre- and post-performance discussion and feedback evaluation of the performance will increase audience enthusiasm, teach the audience theatre techniques, and provide the performers and director with helpful feedback. It also shows the audience they have a valued, respected, and necessary role.

Prior to the performance, explain to the audience a little about the performance and the kinds of poems they will be seeing. Tell the audience that the performers want their feedback.

Ask them to observe how the actors use their imaginations and their voices and movement to become, for example, the graceful moon shedding silver beams or a fussy diner finding a horrible mouse in his stew or a tricky fox trying to feed his family. Ask them to listen to the storytellers and hear what they do with their voices to make the poems enjoyable. Finally ask them to listen to how the sound crew makes their effects crisply and on cue so that they go with the actions of the poems.

After the performance, ask the audience for comments. Make sure all performance elements are mentioned by asking necessary questions. Encourage the audience to write to the performers or draw a picture describing what they liked.

PERFORMERS' REFLECTIONS

Teachers often mention that a performance is one of the year's highlights. Students are naturally excited and buoyed up after the experience. A follow-up reflection helps students articulate what the experience meant to them. It's also a helpful, calming transition to the daily routine of the classroom.

Some possible reflection questions include the following:

- What did you enjoy most about doing this performance?
- What was the most difficult part of the performance for you?
- What was your reaction to having an audience?
- Would you like to do another drama project? Why or why not? If yes, what might it be?

CREATING A CLASS PLAY ALBUM

Students might also make a class album describing and drawing their favorite part of the performance. The album might include copies of tickets, posters, or programs of the show. If the teacher, an aide, or a parent takes photos of all the performers, put them in the album. You might also include notes or pictures from the principal, relatives, or students from other classes.

CHAPTER FIVE

Incorporating Costume Pieces and Rhythm Instruments

Costume is associated with the moving actor
and is the most dynamic and "living" of all the visual designs.
—Francis Hodge, director-author

COSTUME PIECES: THEATRICALIZING THE IMAGERY IN POETRY

COSTUMES AND FABRICS

Costume pieces excite students and make them eager to participate. They help students focus on their role rather than on themselves. Minimal pieces are more stimulating than full costumes because they make students and audiences use their imaginations to fill in the gaps. For example, black fabric draped and tied around the shoulder makes a symbolic raven. White nylon netting creates drifting fog. A baseball cap with ribbons for a mane makes a graceful horse.

INCORPORATING COSTUMES

Tips for incorporating costume pieces are given below. Specific costume suggestions are included with each poem in the book and at the end of the Poetry Performance Script. The Bibliography suggests books on creating simple costumes.

- Keep the costume pieces and props simple, lightweight, unbreakable, and easy to store.
- Find the "telling piece" that captures the tone and feeling for the type of poem dramatized.

- Make sure the costumes are not fragile and that they are easy to put on and take off.
- Keep fabrics light and crushable so they are easy to manipulate and need no ironing.
- Aim for solid colors rather than fabrics with muted colors or busy designs.
- Use everyday objects in a new way. Try a toilet roll as a bird beak or a wooden spoon as a microphone.
- Sort and store costume pieces in boxes by category labeled, for example, Women, Men, Animals, Environment, Fabrics, and Props.
- Let students select fabrics to represent such images as the fog, a crag, or bodies of water. Encourage them to experiment with ways to manipulate the fabric to create the effects desired.
- For a stage performance, do not repeat the same costume piece for different characters in the same production. For example, if there are two birds in different poems, give the duck in one an orange visor and the robin in the other a brown baseball cap.
- Manage costumes for a performance by categorizing them in sturdy clear plastic bags so you can see what you've got.
- For performance, seek help from parents, art teachers, artistic students, and others in the community. Give them credit in the program. The more creative input and involvement you have the richer the production.

COLLECTING COSTUME PIECES AND PROPS

It is exciting to find a prop, fabric, or costume piece that is just right. Beautiful costume pieces and fabrics can be used over and over. For example, a green feather boa around the shoulders makes an enchanting tree or other vegetation. Yellow nylon netting tied around the head can be the sun, a lion's mane, or a daffodil. Blue filmy fabrics make bodies of water and the sky.

Thrift stores, fabric stores, garage sales, parents, friends, and your own castoffs are sources for fabrics, hats, and other pieces.

HATS of all kinds are one of the best ways to help actors assume a character. Some hats can be adapted to suit your purposes. Crushable felt hats are good. Flip up a side, add a feather, and wear it at an angle and you'll have a jaunty Renaissance Shakespearean hat. Turn the brim down, add twigs, gold and silver scouring pads, or some other off-beat object and create a funny old man. Sew on long felt ears to create a dog.

BASEBALL CAPS AND VISORS make animal or bird headpieces. Wear the bill forward to create a critter with a snout or bill. Ears may be attached or you can add white felt eyes on each side with black button centers. Turn the bill around for a turtle or other snoutless critter. Knitted caps or furry hats can be used to create animals' heads.

SHAWLS, LONG SCARVES, AND FEATHER BOAS are theatrical and move well. Shawls with long fringe help create a bird or a feminine damsel. Shawls are good for all types of characterization because they can be manipulated to show nervousness, flightiness, grandeur, or pomposity. Shawls also can be tied around the waist for a theatrical sash or to create a skirt. Scarves can be used to create a variety of headdresses if tied in different ways. Tuck long scarves into pants to make animal tails or hold them between finger tips for butterfly wings. Feather boas may be birds or butterflies too.

GLOVES OR MITTENS can become puppets. Wiggle them to create animated flowers, other vegetation, twinkling stars, butterflies, spiders, or insects. Gloves can also be used to emphasize actions or emotions. Try manipulating your fingers in black gloves to cast a spell or to express power.

APRONS are good for traditional mothers and waiters; delicate frilly ones can be used by feminine little girls.

MAKING NO-SEW COSTUMES

Headband Hats

It is simple to buy or make headbands. For example, fabric trim that can be purchased in fabric stores comes in gold braiding and a variety of patterns and textures. It can be used to create attractive hats by just sewing the ends together.

Paper band hats can be made of different widths. Cut a two-to-three inch wide strip of tagboard long enough to go around the head with an overlap of an inch. Tape or staple the ends together. For a floral crown or seasonal wreath, attach flowers or leaves and ribbon streamers. To create crowns, make a notched or spiked band about six inches wide and decorate it with junk jewelry or bits of foil.

Headband Hats

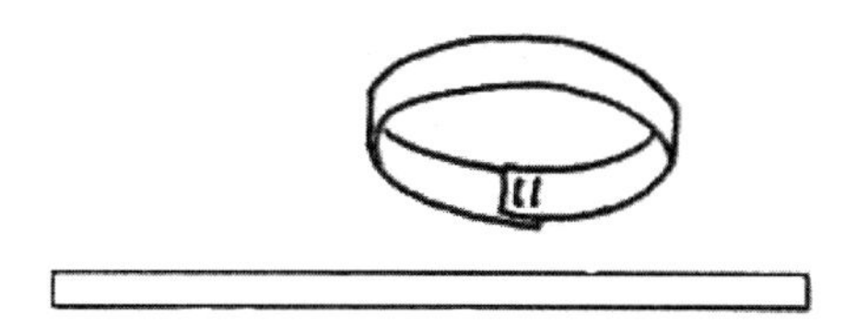

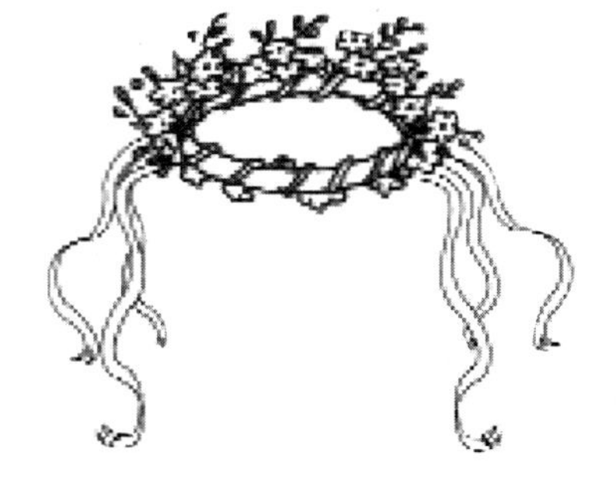

Ceremonial Elastic Band Hats with Height
To create a paper band hat with height for a moon goddess or other ceremonial figure, use poster board about ten inches high and two-inch-wide elastic band for the headband. For a moon goddess, cut a crescent moon about ten inches high of cardboard, cover with silver foil, and attach to the elastic headband. Decorate other hats with pieces of foil, cutouts, ribbons, fabric, or junk jewelry.

Ceremonial Elastic Band Hat with Height

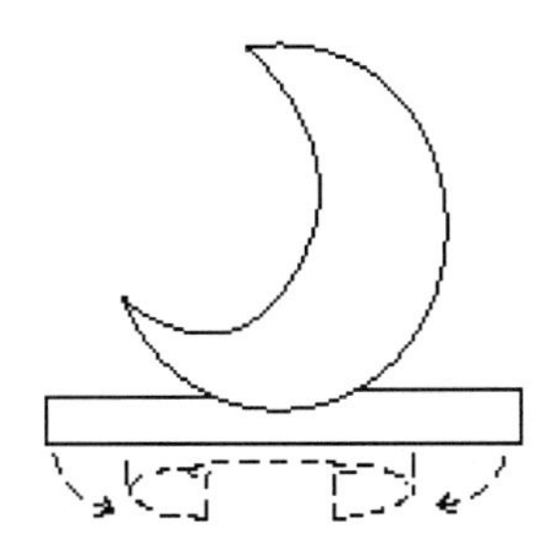

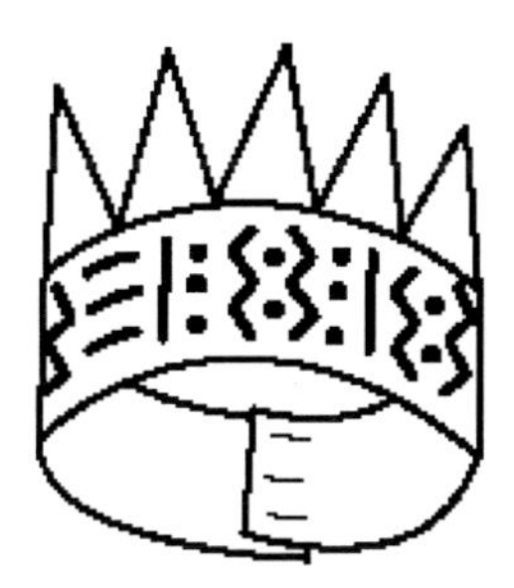

Paper Bag Hats
Paper bag hats can be striking; they are fun and easy to make. Roll up the opening of a brown shopping bag. Place the bag on the head and crush it into the shape and size desired. Paint the bag or leave it plain and decorate it with feathers, bits of fabric, ribbon, or other ornaments. Add animal ears or use foliage such as leaves or twigs to become a tree or a big daffodil. Storytellers might create their own storytelling hats and use them whenever they play the storyteller role.

Paper Bag Hat

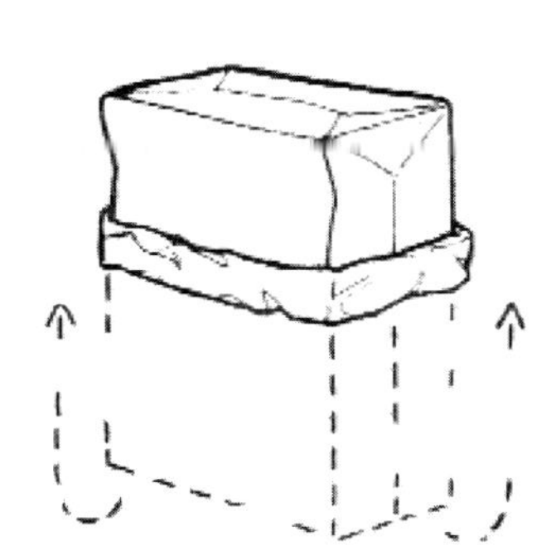

Tunics
Tunics can be used for narrators, storytellers, characters, trees, and objects. For a short tunic (for characters needing free movement), buy one yard of forty-five inch fabric. Fold it in half, and then fold it in half again (quarters). (See diagram.)

Make a three-inch cut for the head. To prevent fraying, apply glue around the opening. (Fray check, available at fabric stores, is good for this purpose.) For a storyteller or long tunic, use two yards of fabric. Tunics can be belted with scarves or sashes.

No-sew tunic

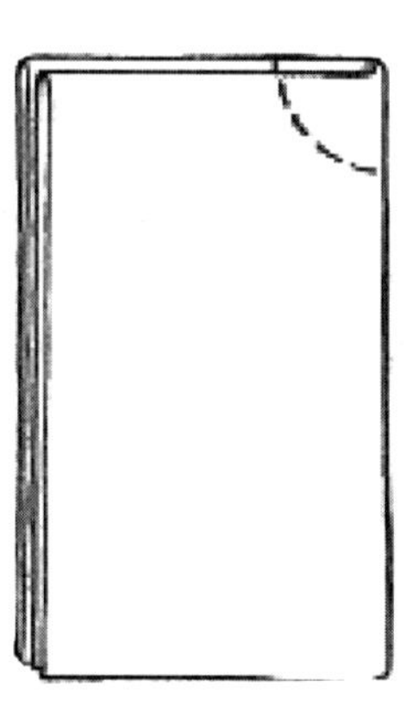

Atmosphere Sticks
Streamers of ribbon, crepe paper, fabric, or other materials can be attached to dowels and waved to create atmospheric effects such as rain, fog, fire, sunshine, or snow. Tape or tie strips of appropriately colored cloth, ribbon, tinsel, or crepe paper to a dowel. Swirling snow needs strips at least two-feet long to create the effect, whereas flames for a fire or the sun's beams might be shorter.

Atmosphere Sticks

Using Fabrics
Fabric can personify nature. Gray fabric held by one or two students can be used for a crag. White nylon netting held becomes fog, clouds, or mist. Filmy fabric can be sky, rivers, seas, and lakes. Collect lightweight fabric such as nylon netting and other sheer fabrics that are easy to manipulate and store.

MUSICAL INSTRUMENTS: EMPHASIZING POETRY'S MUSICAL LANGUAGE

The sounds of the first poems I heard were to me as the notes of bells, the sound of musical instruments.
—Dylan Thomas

The language of poetry is musical. The structure of poetry—its rhythm and rhyme are musical too. Musical instruments heighten and emphasize the music of the language and punctuate the action in poems. Instruments played slowly at the end of a line of poetry slow down the action helping actors and an audience focus on the language and the imagery.

Students are eager to use instruments. Shy and reluctant students not wanting other roles almost always want to play instruments.

INCORPORATING INSTRUMENTS

Tips for incorporating instruments are given below. Specific instrument suggestions are given with many poems—and for every line in poems in the performance script. The Bibliography suggests sources and books on obtaining and creating instruments.

- Model playing instruments to capture the feeling of the language, crisply and on cue.
- Use instruments that suit the tone or feeling of the poem or image.
- To develop musical intelligence, let students select instruments and decide which ones sound best to create the right tone. They may discover, for example, that shaking jingle bells, striking a triangle, or shaking a tambourine lightly all work well to accompany the line "I wandered lonely as a cloud."
- Play instruments at the end of a line of poetry to slow down the action. This helps the audience fully enjoy the image and helps the actors play their roles with artistry and control.
- Acquire the following basic instruments to create many effects: triangle, wood block, jingle bells, drum, tambourine, rattle, and guiro. Buy two or three triangles, wood blocks, jingle bells and rattles for use in groups.
- Buy good quality instruments. They create a better tone, are pleasing to play, and last longer. West Music Company (see Bibliography) has a variety

of instruments at reasonable prices. Also check the Yellow Pages for music supply stores.

USING THE PIANO

A piano might make all the effects if used in a creative way. For example, strike high notes successively to create flying snowflakes, the sailing moon, or a hopping bird. Strike middle notes to resemble hoofbeats, brisk walking, or the eagle clasping a crag. Strike low notes simultaneously or place the heel of your hand on low notes to create a thunderbolt or a character's fall.

Open the piano and strum the strings to highlight the mystery of poems like *Annabel Lee*. Two students might sit at the piano to create the effects. If you or a student play the piano, perhaps experiment with playing music in the background throughout a poem or to accentuate some lines or images. Try lyric poems, such as Thomas Hardy's *The Robin,* Wordsworth's *I Wandered Lonely as a Cloud* or Sandburg's *Fog* using this technique.

MAKING MUSICAL INSTRUMENTS

An interesting assignment is to have students create instruments from everyday objects. This develops musical discrimination as they discover that some coffee mugs, for example, make a pleasant clink when tapped with a spoon and others, an undesirable clunk. Ask students to strike, shake, and scrape objects to test their sounds.

The following suggests simple instruments to make. The Bibliography lists books on making instruments.

RATTLES: Any container with a lid filled with hard objects such as beans, popcorn, or pebbles makes a good rattle. Turn it over, and it's a drum. A large bleach bottle with unpopped corn or beans also works well.

DRUMS: A metal wastebasket struck with a wooden spoon or the hand makes a good drum, or use a coffee can or the bottom of gallon plastic bottle. To make a log drum, remove lids from three juice cans, tape the cans together to make a log shape, and cover with brown grocery wrap. Strike with sticks.

PADDED DRUMSTICK: A ruler or dowel covered with a sock that has another sock stuffed inside of it makes a good drumstick.

RHYTHM STICKS: Use two one-fourth-inch dowels cut one foot long or any two objects of the same size and basic shape, such as a wooden spoon and fork or a metal spoon and fork.

SILVERWARE TAPPERS: Use two forks, knives, or spoons struck together.

GONG: Strike pot lid with a metal spoon.

WOOD BLOCK: Strike a block of wood or even the table or a wall with a pen.

SAND BLOCK: Use a piece of sandpaper scraped with a plastic or metal fork.

BELL: Strike a glass or ceramic coffee cup (with the right bell-like ring to it) with a spoon.

TRIANGLE: Tap or play a glass with the right ping sound by tapping or striking back and forth on the inside with a spoon.

USING OTHER MUSIC

Enhance poetry by using instrumental music to introduce a poem or to play softly in the background while a poem is being recited. Use classical, popular, or folk tunes. Most importantly, the music should in some way evoke and enhance the spirit or tone of the poem.

The music need not be of the time the poem was set although this might add to the authenticity and offer a feeling of the period. For example, try a spiritual or the blues to introduce the poems of Langston Hughes. Use "I've been Working on the Railroad" to introduce *The Ballad of John Henry.* Try Jean Philip Sousa's "Stars and Stripes Forever" to open a program of patriotic poetry. Let students make suggestions.

CREATING VOCALIZED SOUND EFFECTS OR VERBAL EXCLAMATIONS

Gasping, grunting, whining, cheering, and moaning are "emotional calls," and probably were the first forms of speech. These calls are often accompanied by strong body movement to express strong emotion. Vocalized sound effects and verbal exclamations accompanied with expressive movement add vitality to a poetry recitation emphasizing the sound, emotion, and down-to-earth quality of the images and emotions.

This technique works particularly well with nature poetry, nonsense verse, and poems in which characters experience strong emotion. For example in poems with wind, students might sway like the wind saying "SHHHHH" or gyrate vigorously saying "WHOOOSH" depending on the intensity of the storm. The witches in *Macbeth* might cackle to help concoct their evil brew. The characters in *Winter,* might shake saying "Brrrrrrr!" in reaction to the weather. Tigers might bare teeth and growl; gentle lambs, cock heads and baa softly; mysterious owls, open their eyes wide and Whoooo! hauntingly.

Vocalizations and verbal exclamations can punctuate the ending of limericks emphasizing the characters' zany emotional situations and reactions. For example, the old man from Peru might exclaim, "Oh, No!" when he realizes he ate his shoe; the tiger who consumes the lady of Niger might lick his lips, pat his belly exclaiming joyfully, "Yum, yum." The person who ate seeds and broke out in weeds might exclaim "OW!" as he attempts to sit on them.

CHAPTER SIX

Developing English Language and Adapting Poems to Develop English

The medium of poetry is the human voice.
—Robert Pinsky, Poet Laureate

English language learners can learn and enjoy a new language through the complete involvement of poetry dramatization. Dramatization techniques to develop English are described below. For plays, stories, and rhymes, see other books listed in the Literature Dramatization section of the Bibliography, which also has books to develop Spanish language.

VISUAL AIDS

Images in poems are often unusual. Introduce a poem by describing the images and showing pictures of them. Find the right picture of a tiger "burning bright" or daffodils "dancing in the breeze" to introduce a poem and help learners enter the world of the poem. The books, *Talking to the Sun* and *Imaginary Gardens* (listed in the Bibliography), include poems in this book illustrated with art work. *Paul Revere's Ride, The Ballad of John Henry*, and *Annabel Lee* have been completely illustrated in picture books. Other sources of visual aids are wildlife calendars and pictorial history books.

EXAGGERATING THE FOUR SPEAKING SKILLS

To help language learners focus on each word, project strongly and articulate meticulously. Speak slowly and gestures considerably. Speak in an exaggeratedly animated, colorful way.

GESTURING AND BODY MOVEMENT

Gestures help spoken words flow. Slow, repetitive gesturing creates the feeling of the language. Reciting and gesturing creates "muscle memory." To help students remember and experience the language, use slow, clear, enlarged gestures. Exaggerate facial expression.

SYNCHRONIZED GESTURING

In synchronized gesturing, students recite and act the language of the poem; see and hear others recite and act it too. The leader recites the poem and the group dramatizes each line along with the leader. In a more advanced variation, each member of a small group recites and dramatizes a line while everyone dramatizes with the reciter. Even shy students are willing to participate in this pleasant group experience.

INTRODUCING POETRY DRAMATIZATION

Mother Goose rhymes are ideal to begin a program of poetry dramatization with both language learners and English speakers because they are short, humorous, and active. They are full of rhythm and rhyme that teaches the cadence of English speech. Short rhyming poems are easiest to remember and recite.

Mother Goose rhymes also are part of our American literary heritage that all students should know. Their jaunty active humor makes them enjoyable to recite again and again. The following are examples of two Mother Goose rhymes dramatized with an action to do for each line. For more dramatized Mother Goose rhymes, see my book *Dramatizing Mother Goose* listed in the Bibliography.

Jack and Jill went up the hill
(Hold imaginary pail and swing arms up.)
To fetch a pail of water,
(Turn handle of well to draw water.)
Jack fell down and broke his crown,
(Hold head. Say, "OW!")
And Jill came tumbling after.
(Make tumbling motion with arms or spin "In place." Freeze.)

Twinkle, twinkle, little star,
(Raise hand. Open and close it to be a twinkling star.)
How I wonder what you are!
(Open arms out in wonder)

Up above the world so high,
(Arms make circle around head.)
Like a diamond in the sky.
(Fingers of two hands make diamond shape.)
Twinkle, twinkle, little star,
(Raise hand. Open and close it to be a twinkling star.)
How I wonder what you are!
(Raise hand. Open and close it to be a twinkling star.)

SINGING POEMS

Group singing loosens inhibitions and creates energy with a feeling of happy involvement. Some poems are songs. Many Mother Goose rhymes, such as *Jack and Jill, Twinkle, Twinkle Little Star, Baa Baa Black Sheep, Mary Had a Little Lamb,* and *The Noble Duke of York* are often sung. Ballads such as *The Ballad of Mr. Fox* and *The Ballad of John Henry* can be sung too, and, of course, you can use "America the Beautiful" (in the Performance Script). Many have been recorded.

CHOOSING POEMS TO DRAMATIZE

Poetry is excellent to use with language learners. Most useful poems are short. The images are vivid and stimulating. Poems are filled with musical rhythm and many rhyme.

It's unnecessary to completely understand a poem to enjoy it. Indeed, young people's imaginative capacities are stronger and more available to them than their intellectual capacities, so it's natural for them to respond to poetry's language even when they can't understand it intellectually.

Even scholars debate the meaning of poems such as Blake's *The Tyger*, but almost all students respond to the rhythmic power and imaginative use of language as "Tyger, tyger, burning bright."

MEMORIZATION

People can memorize poems before they can read them. After memorizing a poem, students are eager to read it. Begin with Mother Goose rhymes and other short poems and learn a line or couplet a day. By the end of the week, students will know the poem. More advanced students might learn a four-line stanza a day and memorize a longer poem by the end of the week. Copy the poem on large paper and tape it on the door so that they can see it as they leave the room. Use it when teaching them the poem.

MEMORIZATION AND PERFORMANCE

Involved students might perform a memorized poem at the end of the week, using costumes and instruments.

COPYING AND ILLUSTRATING POEMS

Students might copy a short poem or a line from a poem and illustrate it. Put the illustrated poems on the wall and later in loose-leaf notebooks placed in the library or around the room.

ADAPTING POEMS TO DEVELOP ENGLISH LANGUAGE

Chanting words and dramatizing them develops language through repetition and "muscle memory." To adapt poems to this technique, repeat a key word in each line three times and do a gesture to dramatize it. For example, when reciting *Hickory, Dickory Dock,* say "The mouse ran up, up, up the clock" and make your fingers run up one side of your body. Recite "The mouse came down, down, down" and reverse the action.

The following adapts Walter de la Mare's *Someone* and the poem, *How Creatures Move,* to this method.

CAST: (4 to 8. Some may play several roles.) Narrator, Someone, Door, Beetle, Forest, Owl, Cricket, Dewdrops

COSTUME SUGGESTIONS: Black baseball cap turned backwards for beetle; brown, gray, or black hat with one or more gray or brown feathers for owl; black cap with pipe cleaners or other object attached for antenna for the cricket. Silver tinsel on a stick for dewdrops. Someone, Door, and Forest wear all black.

INSTRUMENT SUGGESTIONS: Wood block (for knocking), triangle struck lightly to create mystery, jingle bells as dewdrops fall.

Some One
by Walter de la Mare
Adapted for English Language Learners by Louise Thistle

Some one came knocking, knocking, knocking,
(Knock three times.)
At my wee small door, door, door.
(Arms make door three times.)
Some one came knocking, knocking, knocking
(Knock three times.)
I'm sure—sure—sure.
(Open arms out thinking three times.)
I listened, listened, listened,
(Cup head and bob head rhythmically three times.)
I looked to left and right, left and right, left and right.
(Look left and right.)
But nought there was a-stirring, stirring, stirring,
(Touch lips three times.)
In the still dark night, night, night,
(Stretch arms across body creating night three times.)
Only the busy beetle
Tap-tapping, tap-tapping, tap-tapping, tap-tapping in the wall,
(Tap lightly three times.)
Only from the forest
The screech-owl's call, call, call,
(Cup hands and call three times.)
Only the cricket whistling, whistling, whistling,
(Whistle three times.)
While the dewdrops fall, fall, fall,
(Fingers create falling dew three times.)
So I know not who came knocking, knocking, knocking,
(Shake head and knock.)
At all, at all, at all.
(Shake head mysteriously and rhythmically three times.)

COSTUME PIECE SUGGESTIONS: None. Students use body movement to portray the characters.

RHYTHM INSTRUMENT SUGGESTIONS: Drum, triangle, guiro, tambourine, maracas, wood block

How Creatures Move
Adapted for English Language Learners by Louise Thistle

The lion paws, paws, paws on paws.
(Strike drum.)
The squirrel leaps, leaps, leaps on limbs.
(Strike triangle.)
Flies crawl, crawl, crawl on walls.
(Scrape guiro.)
And seals swim, swim, swim.
(Shake tambourine.)
Worms wiggle, wiggle, wiggle around.
(Scrape guiro.)
The monkey swings, swings, swings by tail.
(Shake maracas.)
Birds hop, hop, hop, on the ground.
(Strike wood block.)
Then spread wings and sail, sail, sail.
(Shake bells.)
But people dancing have fun, fun, fun.
(Shake jingle bells.)
They twist, twist, twist, and run, run, run.
(Shake tambourine and slap it in the center.)

The following is a simpler variation of the poem with less vocabulary and a regular rhythm.

COSTUME PIECE SUGGESTIONS: None needed. Students use body movement to portray the characters.

RHYTHM INSTRUMENT SUGGESTIONS: Drum, tambourine, triangle, guiro, wood block, maracas.

How Creatures Move
By Louise Thistle

A lion paws, paws, paws.
(Strike drum.)
A crow caws, caws, caws,
(Shake tambourine.)
A squirrel leaps, leaps, leaps.
(Strike triangle.)
A bug creeps, creeps, creeps.
(Strike wood block.)
A worm wiggles, wiggles, wiggles.
(Scrape guiro.)
A monkey giggles, giggles, giggles.
(Shake maracas.)
Rabbits hop, hop, hop.
(Strike wood block.)
Tired people flop, flop, flop.
(Strike wood block.)
Let's stop, stop, stop!
(Shake tambourine and slap it in the center.)

CHAPTER SEVEN

A Model Lesson: Nonsense Verse and Tennyson's The Eagle

As a performer, I have become aware of the paradox of my profession. You must be in control and at the same time lose yourself completely.

—Alfred Brendel, classical concert pianist

The following material is a model for teaching poetry dramatization. This introductory lesson using nonsense verse and Alfred Lord Tennyson's *The Eagle* has been done successfully with students of all backgrounds. A complete dramatization of *The Eagle* is on page 51.

The lesson is only a model, of course, and you will want to add or eliminate activities as you see fit. The lesson is designed to involve students quickly and continually in dramatization. This helps them experience the techniques so that they will soon be able to dramatize enjoyably and successfully on their own.

Mother Goose rhymes were chosen to introduce the teaching of speaking skills because they are short and full of action. Most students know them or can easily memorize them. They are part of our cultural heritage with which all students should be familiar. Tennyson's *The Eagle* was chosen to dramatize as a play because it, too, is short and full of action. It is also excellent literature and demonstrates poetic devices to help integrate dramatization with the study of poems as literature. The lesson might be done in one day or over several days.

INTRODUCING THE DRAMATIZATION OF POETRY

MATERIALS

- Chart with the four principles of effective stage speech: **PROJECTION, ARTICULATION, COLORIZATION,** and **SLOW THE PACE.** (Or write these on the board.)
- Chart with Alfred Lord Tennyson's *The Eagle* including symbols of suggested rhythm instruments (as shown below) to play for each line.
- Costume Pieces: Black baseball cap (eagle), gray fabric (crag), blue filmy fabric (sea), yellow nylon netting (sun).
- Rhythm instruments: triangle, wood block, tambourine, guiro, drum.
- List of the following Mother Goose rhymes on the board: *Little Miss Muffet, Humpty Dumpty, Jack Be Nimble, Jack and Jill.*
- Hand bell
- Optional: Pictures of eagles; *Dramatizing Mother Goose* by Louise Thistle (See Bibliography)

The Eagle 

By Alfred Lord Tennyson 

He clasps the crag with crooked hands; 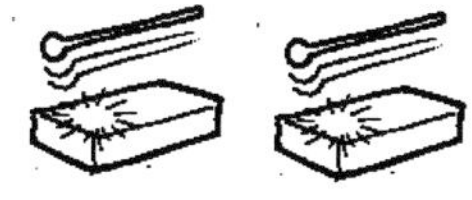

Close to the sun in lonely lands, 

Ringed with the azure world, he stands. 

The wrinkled sea beneath him crawls; 

He watches from his mountain walls, 

And like a thunderbolt he falls. 

GETTING INTO DRAMA AND INTRODUCING THE GOAL

Procedure: Tell students that they will learn techniques to dramatize poetry. First, they will learn and practice the four speaking principles that all good actors and public speakers use to make their material alive and clear. Then, they will practice the principles using nonsense verse. Finally, they will learn how to stage Alfred Lord Tennyson's poem, *The Eagle, as* a play incorporating costume pieces and rhythm instruments. (Display the instruments and costume pieces.)

DISCUSSING THE PRINCIPLES OF GOOD STAGE SPEECH

Procedure: Explain that performers should follow four speaking principles to dramatize poetry effectively. List the principles on the board: PROJECTION, ARTICULATION, COLORIZATION, SLOW THE PACE.

The following exercises require simultaneously chanting the name of each principle and doing a gesture that dramatizes it. Use the bell for control.

DISCUSSING AND PRACTICING PROJECTION

Procedure: Discuss the meaning of projection: throwing your voice out as if you were throwing a ball to the back of a space. Demonstrate by saying "Projection" and throwing an arm out strongly as if you were throwing a ball to the back of the room. Ask how do you feel if a speaker projects poorly? Model poor projection. Mumble a short sentence. Then ask, "What was wrong with the way I spoke then if I were performing for an audience?"

Tell students that when you ring the bell, they will stand and pretend to throw or "project" a ball to the front of the room while chanting PROJECTION four times. Mention the importance of having good posture to use the voice fully.

REINFORCING PROJECTION

Procedure: Mention that the first and most important quality of a good actor is a strong voice. Explain that directors of student plays often look for actors who project well when casting a leading or narrator role.

DISCUSSING AND PRACTICING ARTICULATION

Procedure: Discuss articulation or saying consonants distinctly so that the precise word is understood. Mention that many British actors have excellent articulation so that we know exactly what is being said.

Model poor articulation and then good articulation. Say "cat," slurring the *t.*

Say it again emphatically pronouncing the *t.* Ask students, "What did I do differently the second time to make the word clear?"

Tell them to stand on the bell signal and to point emphatically like a taskmaster to emphasize each syllable, chant AR-TIC-U-LA-TION four times.

REINFORCING GOOD ARTICULATION

Procedure: Ask why articulation is essential in reciting poetry that is short and uses carefully selected words. Practice articulation. Ask students to suggest words that people often don't articulate well such as *going to,* or *want to.*

DISCUSSING AND PRACTICING COLORIZATION

Procedure: Ask students what it means to say that good actors have color in their voices. Describe the vocal technique of colorization: speaking words colorfully to make them sound like what they describe. Demonstrate colorization, having students say the opposite words: *fiery, icy; high, low; huge, tiny; gloom, joy.*

Then, on the bell signal, tell students to stand and chant COLORIZATION four times while opening their arms out in a big colorful gesture.

REINFORCING COLORFUL SPEECH

Procedure: Mention that colorization is the actors' favorite tool to make language and literature come alive. "Colorize" color words. For example, say "green" making it sound like fresh spring green grass. Say "blue" making it sound like a soft blue spring sky. Say "purple," making it sound royal and proud. Say "red," making it vibrate like a new fire engine. Finally, let them choose words to try.

DISCUSSING AND PRACTICING SLOWING THE PACE

Procedure: Discuss the importance of slowing the pace to help an audience hear and fully enjoy the literature and language. Recite *Little Miss Muffet* rapidly. Ask what was wrong with your recitation. Mention that slowing the pace is often essential when reciting poetry to make every word clear.
On the bell signal, have students stand and slowly stretch their arms across their bodies while chanting SLOW THE PACE four times focusing on a slow rate of speech and slowed-down action.

PRACTICING THE FOUR PRINCIPLES

Procedure: Tell students that they will practice the speaking principles using Mother Goose Rhymes that actors use to warm up and practice good speech. Explain that on the bell signal, they will stand and recite *Little Miss Muffet,* with you, practicing the principles. Mention that you will do an action to dramatize each line.

Ring the bell and dramatize *Little Miss Muffet*.

Little Miss Muffet
(Curtsy.)
Sat on a tuffet
(Wiggle to sit.)
Eating her curds and whey;
(Make big scooping motions.)
Along came a spider,
(Walk jaggedly.)
Who sat down beside her,
(Stoop slowly.)
And frightened Miss Muffet away.
(Throw up arms. Freeze.)

Freeze at the end of the rhyme creating a final picture of Miss Muffet with hands thrown up in air, her mouth and eyes wide open in fright. Ring the bell to signal students to sit down.

REINFORCING EFFECTIVE DRAMATIZATION

Praise enthusiastic participation. Next dramatize *Humpty Dumpty*, *Jack Be Nimble, and Rub-a-Dub-Dub* to practice and reinforce the principles.

Humpty Dumpty sat on a wall,
(Become big egg, wobble, and pretend to sit.)
Humpty Dumpty had a great fall.
(Repeat wobble and fall slowly.)
All the king's horses and all the king's men,
(Prance and whinny or slap knees.)
Couldn't put Humpty together again.
(Shake head, shrug, and then freeze.)

Jack be nimble,
(Spin around.)
Jack be quick,
(Run "in place.")
Jack jump over
(Jump.)
The candlestick.
(Point at stick or become a candle and melt slowly.)

Rub-a-dub-dub,
(Swivel hips side to side.)
Three men in a tub,
(Thrust three fingers and head in and out.)
And who do you think they be?
(Shrug rhythmically.)
The butcher,
(Raise imaginary knife high.)
The baker,
(Stir in huge bowl.)
The candlestick maker,
(Raise candlestick in other hand high.)
Toss 'em out, knaves all three.
(Sink to floor holding nose.)

Perhaps dramatize several more rhymes, using my book *Dramatizing Mother Goose* (see Bibliography) or use your own or students' gestures.

PERFORMING *THE EAGLE* AS A PLAY

INTRODUCING THE POEM

Procedure: Tell students they will now stage a serious poem, Alfred Lord Tennyson's *The Eagle* as a play using costume pieces and instruments. Display the costume pieces and instruments.

DISCUSSING EAGLES TO PREPARE TO BECOME ONE

Procedure: Show pictures of eagles. Discuss natural characteristics of eagles and their activities. Mention *The Eagle* is a favorite classic poem poetically describing the behavior of eagles Indicate that the author was a popular poet who enjoyed reciting his poems dramatically.

Procedure: Recite each line of the poem using good articulation and a slow pace. Then, have students recite the line with you.

The Eagle
By Alfred Lord Tennyson

CAST: *Narrator, Eagle, Crag, Sun, Sea (2)*

He clasps the crag* with crooked hands;
(Hands become claws.)
Close to the sun in lonely lands,
(Arms make sun over head.)
Ringed with the azure* world, he stands.
(Lower arms in wide sweeping motion.)

The wrinkled sea beneath him crawls;
(Ripple hands like moving waves.)
He watches from his mountain walls,
(Stretch wings back ready to fly.)
And like a thunderbolt he falls.
(Sweep arms dramatically downwards.)

* steep rugged rock

* the blue of a clear sky

STUDYING THE LANGUAGE AND FIGURES OF SPEECH

Procedure: Discuss the meaning of "crag" and "azure world."

Discuss the Figures of Speech:
  Personification (crooked hands and lonely lands)
  Alliteration (crag/crooked and lonely/lands)
  Hyperbole (close to the sun)
  Simile (like a thunderbolt)

Procedure: With this new knowledge, recite the whole poem with students adding gestures.

STAGING THE POEM

Procedure: Cast the poem choosing students to play the roles and rhythm instruments. Choose an involved, responsible student to play the serious role of the eagle.

Distribute costume pieces: a black baseball cap for the eagle; gray fabric for the crag; dark blue or green-blue filmy fabric for the sea; blue nylon netting for azure world; and gold nylon netting (tied around head) for sun.

Distribute instruments as indicated on the chart. Discuss with students when each is played. Have students practice each effect trying to create the quality of the action depicted.

BLOCKING THE POEM

Procedure: Place actors in the positions that they'll appear in the performance area (probably the front of the classroom) with the goal that all the action is visible and uncluttered.

Place the eagle in the center, the sun on a chair behind him, the crag on one side (kneeling), and the sea on the other side (kneeling or sitting on the floor). The "azure world" will appear behind the eagle and the sun.

Place the Sound Crew in a row along the edge of the stage area so that they are visible to the audience and so that they can see the symbols on the chart and know when to make their sound effects.

EXPLAINING THE NARRATIVE MIME TECHNIQUE

Procedure: Explain that poetry dramatization uses Narrative Mime Dramatization meaning that a narrator recites the poem and the actors act their parts only when the narration says to do so.

For example, when the narrator recites, "He clasped the crag with crooked hands," the crag is formed and behind it the eagle reaches out his talons to clasp it. When that narration is done, the crag and eagle actors freeze so that the audience can focus on the next action about to happen.

STAGING THE OTHER ACTORS' ACTIONS

Procedure: Give the other actors the following actions to do with their lines:

Sun: Close to the sun in lonely lands,
(Raise arms and open them out creating rays.)

Azure World: Ringed by the azure world, he stands.
(Swirl blue netting behind sun.)

Sea: The wrinkled sea beneath him crawls,
(Ripple sea cloth.)

Eagle: Like a thunderbolt, he falls.
(Sweep arms downward and freeze in "plunge" position as the sea cloth is raised perpendicular to simulate the Eagle's disappearing into the sea.)

Review when the instruments should be played referring to the symbols on the chart. Mention too that you will first say "Curtain" to signal that the curtain is going up and the play will begin and that the triangle player will strike the triangle. Then, at the end of the performance you will say "Curtain" again to signal that the curtain is coming down, the play is done, and the triangle will be struck again.

REHEARSING THE ACTION

Procedure: Recite each line slowly as the actors do their actions and the sound crew makes their effects.

PERFORMING THE POEM AS A PLAY

Procedure: Explain that you will narrate, speaking slowly to give performers time to do their actions and time for the audience to enjoy the show.

Recite the poem slowly to allow the actors time to perform artistically, so that the audience can focus and enjoy each image.

EVALUATING THE PERFORMANCE

Procedure: Ask what the actors did specifically that made the drama effective. If someone says he was "a good eagle," ask what the actor did with movement or facial expression to show the power of the eagle. Ask what the sea actors did with the sea cloth to create a "wrinkled sea." Offer your observations to train them in what to observe.

Discuss the sound effects, pointing out how they created effects to simulate the actions. For example, point out how the wood block was played crisply to emphasize the eagle's clasping the crag and how the tambourine was shaken brightly to heighten the sparkling rays. Finally, ask what might be added next time to enhance the performance. Dramatize the poem with different groups of students, pointing how each group of actors brings its own unique creativity to the roles.

INTEGRATING THE DRAMATIZATION OF THE EAGLE *WITH ART*

Procedure: Have students illustrate a favorite line of *The Eagle* and write the line on their paper. Make the illustrations into a class book, having a student write the whole poem in her best writing for the cover or front page.

DRAMATIZING IN GROUPS

MATERIALS

- Copies for students of Christina Rossetti's *Caterpillar,* page 135
- Costume pieces: Brown furry hat for caterpillar; green material over shoulders for leaf and stalk; green baseball cap turned backwards with large eyes attached for frog; yellow baseball cap for bird; white nylon netting draped around body for cocoon, and orange or yellow netting over shoulders as butterfly

INSTRUMENTS: Wood block, rattles, a guiro, and a triangle

Procedure:

- Recite the whole poem. Then, recite the poem again with students. Discuss unknown words and the poem's meaning. Go through the poem line by line having students suggest and demonstrate actions to dramatize each line.

- Divide students into groups of four. Choose one in each group to narrate. Number the roles on the script and assign students to play the roles according to their number. Emphasize that their goals are to recite so everyone can hear and enjoy the poem and to create actions to go with every line.

- Perhaps, give each group one or two instruments and a costume piece to use while practicing in their groups. Mention they can use the instruments and costumes when they perform.

- Allow students 15 minutes to practice (a short time focuses creativity). Ring the bell and students perform. Reinforce those making an effort to speak effectively and groups doing action to dramatize each line. Also have students describe what was done specifically with voice and movement to make the drama effective. Focus on the positive for this first group work.

FOLLOW-UP GROUP PROJECT
DRAMATIZING LIMERICKS

Next, dramatize limericks (Chapter eight). The limericks are good to begin independent group work because they are short and humorous. Gestures are given for every line.

CHAPTER EIGHT

Choosing and Adapting Poems to Dramatize

When people recreate the images through reading and acting,
they have direct contact with the creative images.
—Jack Sanford

Teachers and students may want to dramatize poems other than those in this book. The following describes how to choose and adapt poems.

CHOOSING POEMS TO DRAMATIZE

- Use poems with action. Story poems, ballads, and short nonsense poems have action in most lines. Examples are *Barbara Frieitchie, The Cremation of Sam McGee, The Highway Man, A Froggie Went a Courting* and the poems of Edward Lear, Shel Silverstein, and Ogden Nash.

- Choose excellent literature to which students should be exposed. This literature improves with repetition and is worth the time put into it. The best literature gives students treasures that stay with them all their lives.

- Choose poems from texts including the collected works of poets in this book and other poets. Shakespeare's plays have songs and scenes written in rhyme that are good to dramatize. (For example, this book has the *Double Double Toil and Trouble* scene from *Macbeth* (page 146.) and the song, *Winter,* from *Love's Labor's Lost* (page 149).

- Begin by dramatizing short poems, stanzas, or poems with strong rhythm and rhyme that are especially fun and easy to recite.

ADAPTING POEMS TO DRAMATIZE

- Add action words or make the action word more specific. For example a traditional version of *The Ballad of Mr. Fox* begins, "A fox *came out...*" Change it to: "A fox *trotted out...*" *Trotted* gives students a specific action to do.

- Adapt long poems by using only the stanzas necessary to keep the atmosphere and to tell the story. For example, I adapted Edgar Allan Poe's, *The Raven*, (page168) for this book, condensing the poem from eighteen to eight stanzas.

- Make up a "universal gesture" to act lines with no action. For example to dramatize Emily Dickinson's first line, "Will there eeally be a morning?" raise and open out arms pondering the question.

- Let students suggest gestures if a poem has no action and you don't want to alter it. Students are resourceful in creating gestures to illustrate any line. For example, two students dramatizing the line "I've known rivers," touched their hearts and then wiggled to create rippling rivers.

ADAPTING AND DRAMATIZING A POEM IN GROUPS

Students in groups might adapt poems, deciding which characters and objects to use in their dramatizations and creating actions for each line of a poem.

Procedure: Choose one or more short active poems for groups to dramatize. Assign a student-director for each group to direct the proceedings. To begin, each group member reads a line of the poem. Then, the group decides how to dramatize each line, how many narrators to use and what characters and objects to include in the cast.

Students practice their dramatization revising actions for lines as desired. They practice again and then perform for the class using costumes and rhythm instruments.

SUGGESTIONS FOR CREATING YOUR OWN POETRY PERFORMANCE

This book has a Poetry Performance Script with poems of different types. You may, however, choose to create your own performance using poems of your own choosing.

Choose poems with a variety of moods and styles. Even such serious subjects as Patriotism have a lighter side with song-poems such as "Yankee Doodle Dandy" or "I'm a Grand Old Flag."

Choose poems revolving around a theme such as Patriotism, Black History, Holidays, or the Seasons. Write an introduction that describes the theme and sets the mood. Create transitions between selections or types of selections. (The Poetry Performance Script uses rhyming couplets to introduce each different type of poetry.)

Choose the poetry of one or more poets such as William Shakespeare, Maya Angelou, Emily Dickinson, Langston Hughes, or Christina Rossetti. For Emily Dickinson, Langston Hughes, William Shakespeare, or Christina Rossetti, use the dramatized interviews in this book to introduce their work.

Part II

DRAMATIZING POETRY

CHAPTER NINE

DRAMATIZING LIMERICKS

Speak the speech I pray you as I pronounced it to you trippingly on the tongue.
—Shakespeare

ABOUT LIMERICKS: Limericks are short humorous or nonsense verse that were originally sung. The name comes from Limerick, Ireland, for a reason not fully known. It is probably from a custom at parties in which guests sang a nonsense verse ending with a chorus, "Will you come up to Limerick?"

Limericks first appeared in print in 1820. They became popular in 1846 when poet Edward Lear published his limerick book, *A Book of Nonsense.*

Limericks present zany anecdotes that are ideal to dramatize. The first line introduces the characters and sets the scene. Next, the characters do something, often eccentric. Finally, there's a punch line that often lends itself to slapstick comedy.

Limericks are cleverly written and follow a fixed form. They have five lines. The first two lines rhyme with each other. The third and fourth lines rhyme with each other. But the fifth line must both rhyme with the first two and have a punch that creates surprise. Writers Robert Louis Stevenson, Rudyard Kipling, and Oliver Wendell Holmes are known for limericks. Twentieth-century authors Ogden Nash, W. H. Auden, and David McCord have also written them.

WAYS TO DRAMATIZE

1. Introducing Limericks: Copy limericks for students. Discuss their background. Recite *Limericks Are Lively and Quick*, page 68.
2. Everybody Dramatizes: Recite each line of *An Epicure Dining at Crewe* (emphasizing good articulation), and have students recite each line after you. Recite the whole limerick with students adding gestures. (Dramatize

two or three more limericks the same way. Try *A Flea and a Fly in a Flue* to emphasize articulation.)

3. Pairs or Groups Dramatize: Give pairs or groups a copy of some limericks to dramatize. Students practice and then dramatize for the class. (If acting more than one limerick, groups change narrators so that more students both narrate and act.)
4. Performing: Students bring in costumes, practice again (perhaps using instruments), and perform for others.

Performance Tips:

- Strike a triangle after the title and the author (if there is one) to accentuate each of them.
- After the punch line, freeze the final action, shake a tambourine vigorously and slap it in the center to emphasize the punch.

LIMERICKS ARE LIVELY AND QUICK
By Louise Thistle and Millie Nelson

Limericks are lively and quick.
They come from the place, Limerick.
Each verse has five lines,
And all of them rhyme,
And the rhyming is quite a slick trick.

MODEL: The limerick, *An Epicure Dining at Crewe* gives rhythm instrument and costume suggestions to give students ideas of how they might be performed.

1. AN EPICURE DINING AT CREWE Anonymous
CAST: (3) Narrator, Epicure, Waiter
COSTUME PIECE SUGGESTIONS: *Epicure:* Top hat, *Waiter:* Apron or bow tie

An epicure, dining at Crewe, *(Eat fussily.)*
Shake rattles.
Found quite a large mouse in his stew. *(Look horrified. Hold mouse high.)*
Strike triangle.
Said the waiter, "Don't shout, *(Lean forward, hands on hips.)*
And wave it about, *(Shake finger accusingly.)*
Shake tambourine.
Or the rest will be wanting one, too!" *(Gesture to class and freeze.)*
Shake tambourine and slap it in center.

2. **THERE WAS A YOUNG LADY FROM LYNN** Anonymous, adapted by Louise Thistle
CAST: (2 to 4) Narrator, Lady, Juice bottle or glass (optional)

There was a young lady from Lynn *(Curtsy.)*
Who became so incredibly thin *(Make body skinny.)*
That in bringing her lip
To some juice for a sip *(Pucker lips.)*
She slid down through the straw and fell in. *(Slide down. "Glub, glub.")*

3. **THERE WAS AN OLD MAN FROM PERU** Anonymous
CAST: (2 or 3) Narrator, Old Man

There was an old man from Peru *(Shake, holding cane.)*
Who dreamed he was eating his shoe. *(Lie down. Raise one foot high. Chomp shoe.)*
In the midst of the night *(Sit bolt upright.)*
He awoke in a fright *(Open eyes wide.)*
And—good grief! it was perfectly true. *(Examine shoe. Say, "OH, NO!")*

4. A PIGGISH YOUNG PERSON FROM LEEDS Anonymous
CAST:(2 or 3) Narrator, Old Man

A piggish young person from Leeds (*Rub hands greedily.*)
Made a meal on six packets of seeds (*Reach up and eat six packs.)*
But it soon came to pass *(Examine arms.)*
That he broke out in grass *(Wipe grass vigorously off legs.)*
And he couldn't sit down for the weeds. *(Turn sideways, examine rear end. Say, "OW!")*

5. THERE ONCE WAS A MAN OF BENGAL Anonymous, adapted by Louise Thistle
CAST: (3 or 4) Narrator, Man, Dog

There once was a man of Bengal *(Bow.)*
Who was asked to a cool costume ball; *(Open invitation. Say, "Cool.")*
He murmured: "I'll risk it *(Raise index finger.)*
And go as a biscuit!" *(Become a biscuit.)*
But a dog ate him up in the hall. *(Cover head. Sink to floor.)*

6. THERE WAS AN OLD MAN WHO SAID, "HUSH!" by Edward Lear
CAST: (3 or 4) Narrator, Man, Bird, Bush

There was an Old Man who said, "Hush! *(Put finger by mouth.)*
I perceive a young bird in this bush!" *(Scrutinize bush.)*
When they said—"Is it small?"
He replied—"Not at all! *(Shake head.)*
It is FOUR times as big as the bush." *(Open eyes and arms wide.)*

7. I SAT NEXT TO THE DUCHESS AT TEA Anonymous
CAST: (2 or 3) Narrator, Duchess

I sat next to the Duchess at tea. *(Sip tea.)*
It was just as I feared it would be: *(Wag finger.)*
Her rumblings abdominal *(Pat stomach.)*
Were simply abominable *(Throw arms up.)*
And everyone thought it was ME! *(Eyes wide and point at self.)*

8. **THERE WAS A YOUNG MAID WHO SAID, "WHY?"** Anonymous
CAST(2 or 3): Narrator, Lady

There was a young maid who said, "Why
Can't I look in my ear with my eye? *(Glance toward ear.)*
If I put my mind to it, *(Point to head.)*
I'm sure I can do it, *(Shake finger.)*
You never can tell till you try." *(Shrug.)*

9. **HIGGLETY, PIGGLETY, POP** by Samuel Goodrich
CAST(4 or 5): Narrator, Dog, Cat, Mouse

Higglety, pigglety, pop! *(Spin in one direction on Higglety, the other direction on Pigglety and pop up on Pop.)*
The dog has eaten the mop; *(Chomp mop ravenously "Woof, woof.")*
The pig's in a hurry, *(Run in place, "Oink, oink.")*
The cat's in a flurry, *(Wave paws, "Yowl—eeow.")*
Higglety, pigglety, pop! *(Repeat first line.)*

10. **A BRIDGE ENGINEER, MISTER CRUMPETT** Anonymous
CAST(2 to 4): Narrator, Engineer, Bridge (optional)

A bridge engineer, Mister Crumpett, *(Bow.)*
Built a bridge for the good River Bumpett. *(Arms make bridge.)*
A mistake in the plan
Left a gap in the span, *(Show gap with arms.)*
But he said, "Well, they'll just have to jump it." *(Jump and bow.)*

11. **MISS DOWD AND THE MOUSE** Anonymous, adapted by Louise Thistle
CAST: (3 or 4) Narrator, Miss Dowd, Mouse

A wiggling mouse woke Miss Dowd. *(Wiggle.)*
She jumped up and yelled very loud. *(Jump. "Eeh! Eeh!")*
Then a happy thought hit her: *(Touch head.)*
To scare off the critte, *(Glare, stretch arms out to attack.)*
She stood on her bed and meowed. *("Meow" loudly and freeze.)*

12. **THERE WAS A YOUNG LADY OF NIGER** Anonymous
CAST: (3 or 4) Narrator, Lady, Tiger

There was a young lady of Niger *(Curtsy elegantly.)*
Who smiled as she rode on a tiger. *(Smile broadly, sit sidesaddle on tiger, walk in one direction.)*
They came back from the ride *(Walk next to tiger in other direction.)*
With the lady inside *(Stoop behind tiger who engulfs lady.)*
And the smile on the face of the tiger. *(Grin widely, lick lips. "Yum! Yum!")*

13. **A FLEA AND A FLY IN A FLUE** Anonymous
CAST: (4 to 6) Narrator, Flea, Fly, Flue (one or more)

A flea and a fly in a flue *(Jump, flap wings and use the arms to make flue.)*
Were imprisoned, so what could they do? *(Jump up and down, flap wings.)*
Said, the fly, "Let us flee," *(Raise wing up.)*
Said the flea, "Let us fly," *(Bounce up and down.)*
So they flew through a flaw in the flue.* *(Stoop down and hop and fly out of flue.)*

*Flue (floo): An opening in a chimney to let smoke out.

14. **THERE WAS AN OLD MAN IN A HEARSE** Anonymous
CAST:(2 to 4) Narrator, Man, Hearse (one or two, optional)

There was an old man in a hearse, *(Close eyes, fold arms over chest.)*
Who murmured, "This might have been worse; *(Hand to brow.)*
Of course the expense *(Reach in pocket.)*
Is simply immense, *(Widen arms.)*
But it doesn't come out of MY purse." *(Flip open wallet.)*

15. **THERE WAS A YOUNG MAN NAMED HALL** Anonymous, adapted by Louise Thistle
CAST:(2 to 4) Narrator, Man, Spring (one or two, optional)

There was a young man named Hall *(Bow.)*
Who fell in the spring in the fall. *(Fall.)*
'Twould have been a sad thing *(Shake head sadly.)*
Had he died in the spring, *(Spring up.)*
But he didn't, he died in the fall. *(Fall slowly.)*

16. **THERE WAS AN OLD MAN OF NANTUCKET** Anonymous
CAST: (4) *Narrator, Old Man, Nan, Nan's Man*

There was an old man of Nantucket *(Walk, bent with cane.)*
Who kept all his cash in a bucket; *(Hold up bucket.)*
But his daughter, named Nan, *(Curtsy.)*
Ran away with a man, *(Run "in place.")*
And as for the bucket, Nantucket. *(Grab bucket and run.)*

17. **A DECREPIT OLD GAS MAN NAMED PETER** Anonymous
CAST: (3) Narrator, Peter, Meter (optional)

A decrepit old gas man named Peter, *(Shake cane.)*
While hunting around for the meter, *(Look around.)*
Touched a leak with his light; *(Touch leak.)*
He arose out of sight— *(Arms shoot up.)*
And, as anyone can see by reading or hearing this, he also destroyed the meter. *(Shrug.)*

TOPICS FOR CRITICAL THINKING, WRITING, AND ART

1. Limericks follow a fixed form. How many lines do they have? What is the rhyme scheme, or which lines rhyme with each other?

2. In what way are the beginnings of limericks similar? Find three or four that begin with a similar phrase.

3. Limericks describe unusual behavior. Find two limericks to demonstrate this.

4. Limericks might be read as a kind of joke on occasions, such as someone's birthday or graduation. This is called "occasional verse," written to celebrate a special occasion. What other occasions might be suitable for a limerick? What occasions would not?

5. Students say limericks are funnier acted than read silently. What do they gain from being dramatized?

6. What style of acting best suits a limerick—realistic or broad comedy? Explain. Which actors do you think could best perform limericks?

7. The limerick form has existed many years. What do you think people who enjoy them like about them? Why might someone want to write one?

8. Someone said the success of a limerick depends on its punch line. What does it require to make a good punch line? Is more than just humor required? Explain.

9. Limericks are short, but writers say they are a challenge to write and that it's difficult to write a good one. Study one of your favorite limericks. What does it require to both follow the limerick form and to write a good one?

10. Writing a limerick to dramatize: Offer a prize to the individual, pair, or group that writes the best limerick. Try to think of a first line that ends with a word with lots of possibilities of rhyme, such as *old, hat,* or *cry.* Perhaps, begin with one of the following lines:

    A young man who gulped down his food…

    There was a young woman from…

    A very old dog named Boo Boo…

    Once an amazing old cat…

    A woman who wanted to star…

11. ART: A student said limericks are like verbal comic strips. In what ways, might limericks be like a comic strip? Choose one of your favorite limericks or write your own and illustrate it in a cartoon strip with five panels, one for each line in the limerick.

CHAPTER TEN

Dramatizing Lyrical Poetry

I have just heard a poem spoken with so delicate a sense of its rhythm, with so perfect a respect for its meaning, that if I could persuade people to learn the art I would never open a book of verse again.

—William Butler Yeats

ABOUT LYRICAL POETRY: For the ancient Greeks, a *lyric* was a song expressing emotions such as joy or sorrow. The word *lyric* comes from lyre, a musical instrument (originally made from a turtle shell and several strings) that the ancient Greeks played while someone sang the poem.

The words of songs are still called lyrics, but lyric poems now are usually spoken. Lyric poets make their poems musical by musical effects such as rhyme, rhythm, alliteration, and onomatopoeia. Rather than telling a story, lyric poems often focus on a speaker's feelings about a person, a place, something in nature, or a moment in time. The lyric is the broadest type of verse, and poems that fit no other category are often grouped as lyrics.

Each of the following poems is a lesson that includes About the Poem information, several Ways to Dramatize each poem from the simplest to more complex methods, and Topics for Critical Thinking, Writing, and Art. Lyric poems use many poetic devices referred to in the Topics for Critical Thinking, Writing, and Art. The teacher might copy the definitions of the devices used in the poems on the board from the Glossary in the Appendix for students to refer to.

A SNOWY DAY, *Anonymous*

ABOUT THE POEM: The poem describes the actions of snowflakes and people's reactions to a cold snowy day.

WAYS TO DRAMATIZE

1. INTRODUCING THE POEM: Copy the poem for students. Discuss About the Poem, above.

2. EVERYBODY DRAMATIZES: Recite each couplet and then have students repeat it with you.

3. PAIRS AND GROUPS: Divide the class into Group One and Group Two. As Group One recites the first couplet, Group Two dramatizes it with gestures. Then Group Two recites the next couplet, while Group One gestures, and so forth. Then, divide students into pairs or fours to dramatize the poem. After practicing, some groups could dramatize for the class.

4. PERFORMING: Use instruments and props to perform for others. Perhaps dramatize it with *Winter* by Shakespeare or as part of a program of seasonal poems. (See Subject Index Across the Curriculum.)

CAST: (3 or more) Narrator, Snow, Clouds, Trees, People (2 actors might play all the roles except Narrator).

PROP SUGGESTIONS: *Snow:* Use 18-inch dowels with strips of white crepe paper or ribbon attached to create falling snow.

INSTRUMENT SUGGESTIONS: Shake jingle bells and rattles lightly to emphasize the lyrical action of the snowflakes.

A SNOWY DAY by Anonymous (Adapted by Louise Thistle)

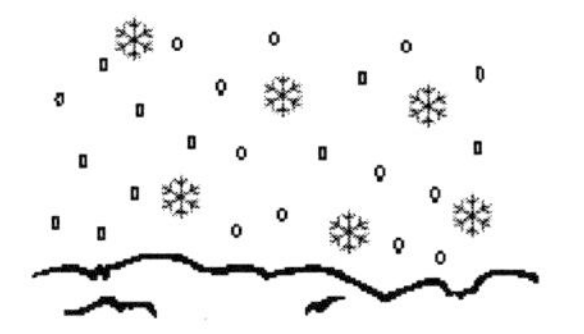

Group 1:
This is how snowflakes sweep about, *(Swirl arms.)*
Among the clouds they fly in an out. *(Twist around.)*

Group 2:
This is how they whirl down the street, *(Spin slowly or arms whirl.)*
Powdering everybody they meet. *(Sprinkle snow.)*

Group 1:
This is how they come fluttering down, *(Hands flutter snow.)*
Whitening the roads, the fields, and the town. *(Powder all areas.)*

Group 2:
This is how snowflakes cover the trees, *(Toss snow onto trees.)*
Each branch and twig bends in the breeze. *(Bend laden with snow.)*

Group 1:
This is how snowflakes blow in a heap, *(Arms make heap.)*
Looking just like fleecy sheep. *(Arms and body collapse into sheep.)*

Group 2:
This is how they cover the ground, *(Spread arms over ground.)*
Cover it thickly, with never a sound. *(Show thickness with arms and hands.)*

Group 1:
This is how people shiver and shake, *(Shiver and shake.)*
On a snowy morning when they first awake. *(Stretch and yawn.)*

Group 2:
This is how snowflakes melt away, *(Arms push away from body.)*
When the sun streams down its beams and rays. *(Arms create sun.)*

TOPICS FOR CRITICAL THINKING, WRITING, AND ART

1. This poem is in rhyming couplets (or couples of lines that rhyme). Tell what the rhyming words are in each stanza. Write a rhyming couplet about the sun.

2. This poem is good to act because all eight stanzas have at least one action verb. Say all the action verbs in each stanza and dramatize each after you say it.

3. Every stanza but one tells the actions of snowflakes. Find the stanza that is not about snowflakes and pantomime the action described in it.

4. The poet begins each stanza with the phrase "This is how…" Why do you think the poet does that? What kind of an effect might the repetition have?

ART: Make traditional snowflakes from a folded square of white paper or make a picture of what you'd like to do on a snowy day.

SUMER IS ICUMEN IN,
by Anonymous (about 1240 A.D.)

ABOUT THE POEM: The poem celebrates the beginning of summer.

WAYS TO DRAMATIZE

1. INTRODUCING THE POEM: Copy the poem for students or write it on the board. Discuss About the Poem, above. Tell students this poem was spoken or sung more than 750 years ago and is in Middle English with words not used today.

2. EVERYBODY DRAMATIZES: Recite each line of the poem. Then have students recite each line with you. Discuss unknown words. Reword the poem in Modern English. Then, recite the original poem again with students adding gestures.

3. PAIRS OR GROUPS DRAMATIZE: Divide the class into three groups with each reciting its designated line and everyone reciting the Chorus "cuccu" lines.

4. PERFORMING: Use instruments and costume pieces and perform for others. Perhaps dramatize it with the other seasonal poems in this book. (See Subject Index Across the Curriculum.)

COSTUME SUGGESTIONS: *Summer:* Artificial flowers to emphasize "Sumer is icumen in"; *Cuccu:* Gray baseball cap; *Med*: Sheaves of wheat

INSTRUMENT SUGGESTIONS: Shake jingle bells for "bloweth med," strike triangle for "sprigget the wude nu."

SUMER IS ICUMEN IN, Anonymous
adapted by Louise Thistle

Group 1:
Sumer is icumen* in: *(Thrust arms up.)* *coming

Chorus:
Lhude* sing cuccu! cuccu! *(Tilt head back. Sing "Cuccu" joyfully.)* *loud

Group 2:
Growethe sed,* and bloweth med,* *(Arms sway.)* * seed *meadow

Group 3:
And springth* the wude* nu* *(Thrust arms up.)* *springs *new

Chorus:
Sing cuccu! cuccu! *(Tilt head back. Sing "Cuccu" joyfully.)*

TOPICS FOR CRITICAL THINKING, WRITING, AND ART

1. This poem was recited hundreds of years ago, yet people like to recite it today. Recite the poem. What parts of the poem do you like to recite?

2. The word *cuccu* uses ONOMATOPOEIA meaning that the word *cuccu* sounds like the sound the bird makes. In what way does the word *cuccu* also express the lighthearted, fun-loving spirit of summer? What ONOMATOPOETIC words might you use to express the spirit of cold winter?

3. Rewrite the poem to fit another event or season. For example, to celebrate the beginning of the weekend and Thanksgiving, two writers wrote:

   Weekend is icumen in;
   Sing, Whoopee!
   Get up late. Lots of dates
   And feeling nice and free
   Sing, Whoopee!

   Thanksgiving is icumen in
   Sing Turkey
   Football games and bonfire flames
   Feeling quite sprightly
   Sing, Turkey!

ART: In the days before the printing press (at the time this poem was recited), monks wrote books by hand. The first letter in these books was drawn in a large elaborate design. Why do you think they did this? Design a fancy or elaborate *S* to begin this poem. Then, write the rest of the poem using your best printing.

THE LAMB *by William Blake (1757–1827)*

ABOUT THE POEM: William Blake made his living by giving drawing lessons and illustrating books, including his own books *Songs of Innocence* and *Songs of Experience. The Lamb* comes from *Songs of Innocence.*

WAYS TO DRAMATIZE

1. INTRODUCING THE POEM: Copy the poem for students. Discuss About the Poem, above.

2. EVERYBODY DRAMATIZES: Recite each line of the poem using good articulation and speaking slowly. Then students recite each line with you. Recite the whole poem with students adding gestures.

3. PAIRS OR GROUPS DRAMATIZE: Divide the class into pairs or groups of four to dramatize the poem. Some groups might choose to use several narrators. Some might choose to gesture as a group chorus, as one or more narrators recite each line. Some groups may be chosen to dramatize for the class.

4. PERFORMING: Use costumes and instruments. Perform the poem for others, perhaps with *The Tyger* (page 86) to experience Blake's "two contrary states of the human soul."

CAST: *(2)* Narrator, Lamb. Others might dramatize (doing the gestures) as a chorus or play instruments.

COSTUME SUGGESTIONS: *Lamb:* White wooly hat (perhaps with ears attached)

INSTRUMENT SUGGESTIONS: Triangle, rattle, jingle bells, sand blocks, and wind chimes.

THE LAMB by William Blake

Little Lamb, who made thee? *(Open arms out questioning.)*
Strike triangle.
Dost thou know who made thee? *(Shake head.)*
Strike triangle.
Gave thee life and bid thee feed *(Raise arms on "life." Touch lips on "feed.")*
Shake rattle.
By the stream and o'er the mead;* *(Arms make stream and gesture to "mead.")*
Shake jingle bells.

*mead: meadow

Gave thee clothing of delight, *(Show arms.)*
Shake rattle.
Softest clothing wooly bright; *(Rub cloth.)*
Scrape sand blocks.
Gave thee such a tender voice, *(Touch lips.)*
Say "Baa" softly.
Making all the vales* rejoice! *(Reach forward.)*
Jingle bells.

*valleys

Little Lamb, who made thee? *(Repeat first two lines.)*
Strike triangle.
Dost thou know who made thee?
Strike triangle.
Little Lamb, I'll tell thee, *(Point finger gently.)*
Strike triangle.
Little Lamb, I'll tell thee! *(Repeat.)*
Strike triangle.
He* is called by thy name, *(Point to lamb.)*
Shake wind chimes.

*Christ

For he calls himself a Lamb; *(Gesture to sky.)*
Shake wind chimes.
He is meek and he is mild, *(Bow head.)*
He became a little child; *(Rock baby.)*
Jingle bells.
I a child and thou a lamb, *(Point to self and lamb.)*
Jingle bells.
We are called by his name. *(Point to self and lamb.)*
Shake wind chimes.
Little lamb, God bless thee. *(Put hand over lamb's head.)*
Strike triangle.
Little lamb, God bless thee. *(Repeat.)*
Strike triangle.

TOPICS FOR CRITICAL THINKING, WRITING, AND ART

1. What did the Creator give the lamb in the second stanza that makes the animal delightful?

2. In what way is the lamb in the poem like a real lamb? In what way is he a SYMBOL of something other than a real lamb? What does he symbolize?

3. The lamb in the poem is "meek and mild." What do "meek and mild" mean? Are these good qualities to have? Explain.

4. Repeated lines create RHYTHM and add emphasis. Find the lines the poet repeats and say them aloud.

5. What is the speaker in the poem's attitude toward the lamb?

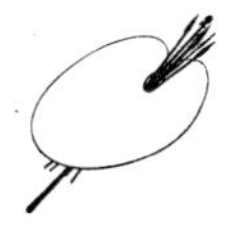

ART: Cut out or tear a lamb from white paper. Perhaps color the face black.

THE TYGER *by William Blake (1757–1827)*

ABOUT THE POEM: *The Tyger* comes from William Blake's *Songs of Experience* and describes the great power and force of a tiger. The speaker questions what type of Creator could have made an animal of such fearsome power and force.

WAYS TO DRAMATIZE

1. INTRODUCING THE POEM: Copy the poem for students. Discuss About the Poem, above, comparing the poem to *The Lamb*, page 84.

2. EVERYBODY DRAMATIZES: Recite each stanza of the poem using good articulation and speaking slowly. Have students recite each stanza after you. Then, recite the whole poem with students adding gestures.

3. PAIRS OR GROUPS DRAMATIZE: Divide the students into groups to dramatize the poem. Some groups may be chosen to dramatize for the class.

4. PERFORMING: Use costumes and instruments. Perform the poem for others along with *The Lamb* (page 84) to experience Blake's "two contrary states of the human soul."

CAST: (4 or more) Narrator, Tyger, Forest

COSTUME SUGGESTIONS: *Tyger:* Black clothing. Shimmer gold tinsel on a dowell for "burning bright" and "burnt the fire of thine eyes"; *Forest*: All black clothing

INSTRUMENT SUGGESTIONS: Use a light background drum beat throughout the poem.

THE TYGER by William Blake

Tyger! Tyger! burning bright *(Say powerfully. Hands make fire.)*
In the forests of the night, *(Arms create trees.)*
What immortal hand or eye *(Show hand. Touch an eye.)*
Could frame thy fearful symmetry?* *(Arms create frame. Crouch and snarl.)*

* symmetry: the proper proportions of the parts of the body or whole to one another with regard to size and form.

In what distant deeps or skies *(Reach down, then up.)*
Burnt the fire of thine eyes? *(Scowl fiercely.)*
On what wings dare he aspire? *(Raise powerful wings.)*
What the hand dare seize the fire? *(Hold up hand, seize fire, and shimmer.)*

And what shoulder, and what art, *(Point to powerful shoulders. Then, point to head.)*
Could twist the sinews of thy heart? *(Twist hands near heart.)*
And, when thy heart began to beat, *(Hand beats slowly on heart.)*
What dread hand? and what dread feet? *(Show powerful hand. Gesture to feet.)*

What the hammer? what the chain? *(Raise hammer. Hands show chain.)*
In what furnace was thy brain? *(Hands create furnace. Hold temples.)*
What the anvil?* what dread grasp *(Hold anvil and grasp mightily.)*
Dare its deadly terrors clasp? *(Make fists.)*

* anvil: heavy iron block on which metals are hammered into shape

When the stars threw down their spears,* *(Throw stars down.)*
And watered heaven with their tears, *(Hands create falling rain.)*
Did he smile his work to see? *(Smile. Nod head.)*
Did he who made the lamb make thee? *(Pat lamb. Point to tiger.)*

* stars...spears: a reference to the angels who fell with Satan and threw down their spears after losing the war in Heaven.

Tyger! Tyger! burning bright *(Repeat actions of first stanza.)*
In the forests of the night,
What immortal hand or eye,
Dare frame thy fearful symmetry?

TOPICS FOR CRITICAL THINKING, WRITING, AND ART

1. *The Tyger* uses APOSTROPHE, talking to the tyger as if he were present. What questions is the speaker asking the tyger?

2. Why does the poet refer to the tyger as "burning bright"?

3. Why does the poet repeat the first stanza at the end?

4. How does the speaker feel about the tyger?

5. The poet uses ALLITERATION, words close together that begin with the same consonant sound. Find examples of ALLITERATION.

6. The tyger is an animal, but he is also a SYMBOL meaning something more than a real tyger. What do you think the tyger might symbolize?

7. Henri Rousseau painted a striking picture of a tiger called *The Surprise.* Find a copy of the picture. What is the tiger's attitude in Rousseau's painting?

8. Write a poem in which you talk to or address another animal—or anything in nature—and ask it where it got its attributes.

ART: Draw contrasting scenes of the two poems, *The Lamb* and *The Tyger.* Or draw the tyger "burning bright."

IN JUST- *by e.e. cummings (1894–1962)*

ABOUT THE POEM: Spring just begins. The children play active games and see the little lame balloonman whistling "far and wee."

WAYS TO DRAMATIZE

1. INTRODUCING THE POEM: Copy the poem for students. Discuss About the Poem. Ask students to listen for unusual words describing the feeling of spring. Recite the poem.

2. EVERYBODY DRAMATIZES: Have students stand and recite the poem while you do the gestures.

3. PAIRS OR GROUPS DRAMATIZE: Cast a group of students to dramatize the poem as a play. Perhaps have the audience sit around the edge of a circle and the actors enter into the circle to play their roles. Then, divide the class into groups to dramatize the poem. Some groups may be chosen to dramatize for the class.

4. PERFORMING: Use costume pieces and instruments and perform for others—perhaps with Wordsworth's *I Wandered Lonely as a Cloud* (another spring poem) or other seasonal poetry. (See Subject Index Across the Curriculum.)

CAST: (6 or 7) Narrator, Balloonman, Eddie, Bill, Betty, Isabel

COSTUME SUGGESTIONS: *Eddie, Bill, Betty, and Isabel:* Appropriate children's hats; *Balloonman*: Peaked green Peter Pan–style hat and one or more balloons.

INSTRUMENT SUGGESTIONS: Use jingle bells, a wood block, and a triangle to accent the action. Balloonman might whistle or use a panpipe.

IN JUST- by e.e. cummings

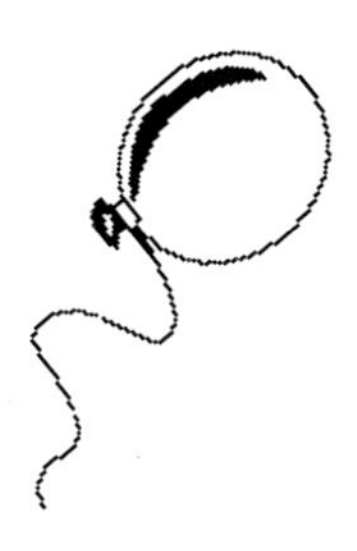

In just-
spring when the world is mud— *(Plod through mud.)*
luscious the little
lame balloonman *(Limp.)*

whistles far and wee* *(Whistle.)*

*tiny

and eddieandbill come
running from marbles and *(Run "in place.")*
piracies and it's
spring *(Toss arms up.)*

when the world is puddle-wonderful *(Jump over puddles.)*

the queer
old balloonman whistles *(Whistle.)*
far and wee
and bettyandisbel come dancing *(Skip.)*

from hop-scotch and jump-rope and *(Hop and jump.)*

it's
spring *(Toss arms up.)*
and
the
goat-footed *(Hobble.)*

balloonMan whistles *(Whistle.)*
far *(Stretch arms forward.)*
and
wee. *(Pull arms to chest.)*

TOPICS FOR CRITICAL THINKING, WRITING, AND ART

1. The poet, e. e. cummings, was a painter and a poet. In this spring poem, he uses IMAGES (or word pictures) of spring. What are some of the pictures he paints with words of spring?

2. What makes mud "luscious" to children? Why are puddles "puddle-wonderful" for children?

3. Find unusual capitalization, punctuation, and spacing of words and tell why you think the poet used them.

4. Why is the poem one long run-on sentence without a period until the last word?

5. Some people believe the balloonman is a modern version of the ancient Greek God Pan who played a panpipe, was a god of forests and pastures, and who had the feet and legs of a goat. What in the behavior of the balloonman makes him like the Greek God Pan? Find a picture of Pan or read one of the Greek myths about him. Is he a serious or light-hearted character? Explain.

ART: Cut out balloon shapes from colored paper and tape or tie a string on them. Print a phrase or image in the poem that you like on your balloon. Display the balloons on a bulletin board. Or draw a picture of one or more scenes from the poem. Write the words of the poem that go with it.

INTERVIEW (1830–86) WITH MABEL TODD, FRIEND OF EMILY DICKINSON'S BROTHER, AUSTIN

(Based on letters that Mabel Todd wrote to her parents about Emily Dickinson in the 1880s.)

WAYS TO DRAMATIZE

1. INTRODUCING THE AUTHOR: Give students the interview. Tell students to listen to the description of Emily Dickinson (given by Mabel Todd). Read the interview aloud. Ask students to describe the two women and tell why Mabel Todd wanted to get Emily Dickinson's poems published.

2. PAIRS DRAMATIZE: Divide students into pairs to act the two roles. Choose two students to dramatize the interview for the class.

3. PERFORMING: Use costume pieces and props and perform the interview with poems by Emily Dickinson from this and perhaps other books.

CAST: TV (2) Interviewer (lively, animated); Mabel Todd: (confident, convinced of the excellence of Emily Dickinson's poetry and eager to promote it).

COSTUME SUGGESTIONS: *Mabel Todd:* Tasteful velvet hat of the late 1800s. *Woman TV Announcer:* Bright, solid-colored blazer with tasteful blouse and perhaps a scarf. *Male TV Announcer:* Jacket and tie, spatula or wooden spoon for microphone.

TV Announcer: *(Heartily.)* Good Evening, TV viewers. We've been trying for years to get Emily Dickinson onto the *Meet the Poets* show. Since Miss Dickinson hasn't left her house for twenty years, I guess that attempt was bound to fail. But, we do have Mabel Todd, a friend of her brother, Austin, and the person who was the most instrumental in getting Emily Dickinson's poems published for the world to appreciate. Welcome, Mrs. Todd, to *Meet the Poets.* Mrs. Todd, why hasn't Emily Dickinson left her house for twenty years?

Mabel Todd: Actually, she did go out once. She crept out at night when everyone was asleep to see the new church by moonlight. Only her mother and sister see her. Once in a while, she allows little children to come in one at a time, and she gives them cake or candy.

TV Announcer: How did you meet her?

Mabel Todd: Her sister, Vinnie, asked me to come to sing and play the piano. Emily would hide behind the door to listen while I was playing, but I never saw her.

TV Announcer: Doesn't that seem odd to you?

Mabel Todd: *(A bit impatiently.)* Of course, it seems odd. But the ways of a genius seem strange to most of us. Once, as a young woman, Emily went to Washington, D.C. to visit her father who was a Congressman. After she saw what was going on there, her brother Austin said that she felt that a life like that was hollow in comparison to her rich inner world. So, she never left her home again.

TV Announcer: And you said she then dedicated her life to words. What does that mean?

Mabel Todd: "Words," she told me, "are my life." She looked on words as very powerful. She wrote once that poets must choose but a few words, and they must be "the chiefest ones."

TV Announcer: *(Perplexedly.)* The chiefest ones?

Mabel Todd: The most important, appropriate, and exact word to suit the situation she wanted to express. Study her poems you'll see what she means.

TV Announcer: O.K., I will right after the show. But you know when Emily died in 1886 at the of age fifty-six, only seven of her poems had been published anonymously. And, in fact she wrote 1,775 poems. If they were so good, why weren't they published during her lifetime?

Mrs. Todd: At the time, people didn't understand them. They are unique. They have unusual rhymes, and they challenge the reader.

TV Announcer: How did you get involved in Emily's poetry?

Mrs. Todd: Even though I am quite a social person, I felt closer to Emily and what she was trying to say than I EVER did with my socialite friends. Getting her poems published was a wonderful experience for me. It gave my life meaning and purpose to bring this wonderful poet into the world for everyone to appreciate.

TV Announcer: That is remarkable.

Mrs. Todd: Emily Dickinson's poems are what's remarkable.

TV Announcer: Yes, Emily Dickinson might have thought of herself as she said in one of her poems as an anonymous NOBODY. But clearly she is truly a SOMEBODY now known by literature lovers throughout the world. Thank you, Mrs. Todd for appearing on *Meet the Poets* and illuminating this extraordinary poet for us.

Mabel Todd: It was a pleasure to spread the word on someone who changed my life, and thank you for your interest.

A BIRD CAME DOWN THE WALK
by Emily Dickinson (1830–86)

ABOUT THE POEM: The speaker carefully observes a bird eating, drinking, and looking around for danger and then tries to feed it.

WAYS TO DRAMATIZE

1. INTRODUCING THE POEM: Copy the poem for students. Discuss About the Poem, above, and the interview about Emily Dickinson as needed. Ask students to focus on the actions the bird does in the poem. Recite the poem using good articulation and a slow pace.

2. EVERYBODY DRAMATIZES: Recite the poem line by line doing gestures, and ask students to echo you.

3. PAIRS OR GROUPS DRAMATIZE: Divide the class into groups to dramatize the poem as a play.

4. PERFORMING: Using costume pieces and instruments, perform the poem with the interview and other poems by Emily Dickinson in this and other books.

CAST: (3 or more) Narrator, Bird, (one or as many as desired to play Beetle, Grass, Oars, and Butterfly)

COSTUME SUGGESTIONS: *Bird:* Solid-colored baseball cap; *Worm*: Brown cap; *Beetle:* Black cap

INSTRUMENT SUGGESTIONS: Use a triangle, wood block and jingle bells to accent the bird's actions.

A BIRD CAME DOWN THE WALK by Emily Dickinson

A Bird came down the Walk— *(Hop lightly.)*
He did not know I saw— *(Shake head.)*
He bit an Angleworm in halves *(Bite.)*
And ate the fellow, raw, *(Tilt head back, swallow.)*

And then he drank a Dew *(Poke bill down drinking.)*
From a convenient Grass— *(Fingers make wiggling grass.)*
And then hopped sideways to the Wall *(Hop.)*
To let a Beetle pass— *(Gesture letting it pass.)*

He glanced with rapid eyes *(Blink eyes, bob head.)*
That hurried all around— *(Look around nervously.)*
They looked like frightened Beads, I thought— *(Blink rapidly.)*
He stirred his Velvet Head *(Turn head slowly.)*

Like one in danger, Cautious, *(Stoop cautiously.)*
I offered him a Crumb *(Hold out crumb.)*
And he unrolled his feathers *(Stretch out wings.)*
And rowed him softer home— *(Flap wings dreamily.)*

Than Oars divide the Ocean, *(Dip and fly "in place.")*
Too silver for a seam—
Or Butterflies, off Banks of Noon *(Flutter wings.)*
Leap *plashless as they swim. *(Fly and freeze.)*

*without making a splash

TOPICS FOR CRITICAL THINKING, WRITING, AND ART

1. The poet uses a SIMILE comparing the bird's eyes to "frightened Beads." In what way might a bird's eyes look "like frightened beads"?

2. What is the bird's attitude toward the angleworm?

3. What is the bird's reaction when the speaker offers it a crumb?

4. Why do you think the speaker was "Cautious" when she offered the bird a crumb?

ART: Illustrate one of the bird's actions.

A WORD IS DEAD *by Emily Dickinson (1830–86)*

ABOUT THE POEM: The speaker describes a word as a living thing.

WAYS TO DRAMATIZE

1. INTRODUCING THE POEM: Copy the poem for students. Discuss About the Poem, the interview with Mabel Todd, and other Dickinson poems as needed.

2. EVERYBODY DRAMATIZES: Recite each line of the poem slowly using a dark heavy voice for Speaker One, and a light, bright voice for Speaker Two. Students repeat each line with you. Then, recite the whole poem with students adding gestures.

3. PAIRS OR GROUPS DRAMATIZE: Divide the class into two groups. Group One plays Speaker One (speaking in a heavy voice) and Group Two, Speaker Two (speaking in a light, bright voice). Reverse the roles. Dramatize the poem in pairs.

4. PERFORMING: Use props and instruments and perform to others perhaps using the interview and other Dickinson poems.

CAST: (2) Speaker 1, Speaker 2

PROP SUGGESTIONS: Print words on cards and manipulate them to suggest they are dead or alive.

INSTRUMENT SUGGESTIONS: Strike wood block rapidly for dead word and shake jingle bells brightly for live word.

A WORD IS DEAD by Emily Dickinson

Speaker One:
A Word Is Dead

Speaker Two:
By Emily Dickinson

Speaker One: *(Heavily.)*
A word is dead *(Head and arms hang down.)*
When it is said, *(Cup hands to mouth.)*
Some say. *(Head down.)*

Speaker Two: *(Brightly.)*
I say it just *(Point to self.)*
Begins to live *(Spin.)*
That day. *(Raise arms up triumphantly.)*

TOPICS FOR CRITICAL THINKING, WRITING, AND ART

1. In this poem "a word" is compared to a person as being dead or alive using PERSONIFICATION. In what way is "a word" in the poem like a person? Say the word "angry" making your voice sound like an angry person. Say "joy" making your voice and body express a person feeling great joy.
2. The speaker believes spoken words have power and life. In what way might something you say to someone change the feeling they have about themselves and the world? Give an example of something positive someone said to you that brightened your life. How might words damage a person's esteem?
3. The speaker skillfully reveals her feeling (about saying words) in a poem of only nineteen words. The rhyming is unusual in this poem too. Where are the rhyming words in the poem?
4. Some scholars say that spoken words are more "real" than written words. Why do they say this? Which do you think are more "real"? Explain.

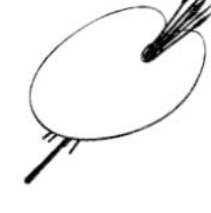

ART: Draw a cartoon showing words that come alive.

I'M NOBODY! WHO ARE YOU?
by Emily Dickinson (1830–86)

ABOUT THE POEM: The speaker says she is a Nobody. And she describes the Somebody who seeks constant fame and attention.

WAYS TO DRAMATIZE

1. INTRODUCING THE POEM: Copy the poem for students. Discuss About the Poem, the interview with Mabel Todd, and other Dickinson poems as needed.

2. EVERYBODY DRAMATIZES: Recite each line of the poem and then have students recite the line with you.

3. PAIRS OR GROUPS DRAMATIZE: Divide the class into two groups. Group One plays Speaker One and Group Two, Speaker Two. Reverse the roles. Then, divide the class into pairs to play Speakers One and Two. Some groups may be chosen to dramatize for the class.

4. PERFORMING: Use costume pieces and perform the poem for others, perhaps with the interview and other Dickinson poems.

CAST: (4 or more) Speaker One, Speaker Two, Frog-like persons (2 or more)

COSTUME SUGGESTIONS: *Speaker One and Speaker Two (The Nobodys):* use black half-masks or wear big name tags saying NOBODY; *Frog-like persons:* Green baseball caps turned backwards.

I'M NOBODY! WHO ARE YOU? by Emily Dickinson

Speaker One:
I'm Nobody! Who Are You?

Speaker Two:
By Emily Dickinson

Speaker One:
I'm Nobody! Who are you? *(Point to self and then to audience.)*

Speaker Two:
Are you—Nobody—too? *(Open arms out in question.)*

Speaker One:
Then there's a pair of us! *(Raise two fingers.)*

Speaker Two:
Don't tell! they'd banish us—you know! *(Finger by lips, "Shh.")*

Speaker One:
How dreary—to be—Somebody! *(Hang head.)*

Speaker Two:
How public—like a Frog— *(Chest out.)*

Speakers One and Two:
To tell your name—the livelong June

Speakers One and Two:
To an admiring Bog.* *(Squat. Say, "Ribbet.")*

*bog: wet ground with soil made of decayed vegetable matter

TOPICS FOR CRITICAL THINKING, WRITING, AND ART

1. The speaker says "I'm Nobody." From the poem's point of view is being a Nobody a bad thing to be? Explain.

2. The poem uses a SIMILE comparing being a Somebody to being "like a Frog." Dramatize the SIMILE by becoming a person with the voice of a frog. How is a frog's voice like that of a boastful person?

3. Emily Dickinson capitalizes words that are not at the beginning of lines and are not proper names. She uses dashes in punctuation unusually. Recite the poem. Explain why she might capitalize the words she does and why she uses dashes where she does.

ART: Draw a cartoon of your idea of a Nobody, a Somebody, or both.

WILL THERE REALLY BE A MORNING?
by Emily Dickinson (1830–86)

ABOUT THE POEM: The speaker wonders if there is anything that you can see in the world that explains exactly what the words *morning* and *day* are.

WAYS TO DRAMATIZE

1. INTRODUCING THE POEM: Copy poem for students. Discuss About the Poem, above. Ask students to listen for the unusual way the poet has of trying to understand what morning and day are. Recite the poem focusing on good articulation and speaking at a slow pace.

2. EVERYBODY DRAMATIZES: Recite each line of the poem, and have students recite each line with you. Then, recite the whole poem slowly with students adding gestures.

3. PAIRS OR GROUPS DRAMATIZE: Divide the students into pairs: One recites and the other gestures. Or dramatize the poem in groups using the cast list. Some groups may be chosen to dramatize for the class.

4. PERFORMING: Use instruments and dramatize the poem perhaps using the interview and other Dickinson poems.

CAST: (2 or more) Narrator, Person, Water lilies, Bird, Scholar, Sailor, Wise Man from Skies (The Person might dramatize all of the inanimate objects or use several actors.)

INSTRUMENT SUGGESTIONS: Strike a triangle to emphasize the images in the poem.

WILL THERE REALLY BE A MORNING? by Emily Dickinson

Will there really be a morning? *(Make rising gesture.)*

Is there such a thing as day? (*Open arms out in wonder.)*

Could I see it from a mountain *(Shade eyes.)*

If I were as tall as they? (*Arms make peak.)*

Has it feet like water lilies? *(Hands become bobbing lily pads.*)

Has it feathers like a bird? *(Flutter wings.)*

Does it come from far off places *(Shade eyes, gesture far off.)*

Of which I've never heard? *(Shake head.)*

Oh, some scholar! Oh some sailor! *(Put thumb under chin thinking. Then, salute.)*

Oh some wise man from the skies *(Gesture to sky.)*

Please do tell this little pilgrim *(Bow.)*

Where the place called morning lies. *(Make rising gesture.)*

TOPICS FOR CRITICAL THINKING, WRITING, AND ART

1. Which lines in the poem rhyme?

2. What questions does the speaker ask?

3. Why do you think the poet can't find answers to her questions?

4. People have wondered why the speaker in this poem asks these questions. What do you think this poem means? Why do you think the speaker asks these unusual questions?

5. Emily Dickinson uses language in an unusual way. For example, she says water lilies have "feet." What are the "feet" that she means?

6. Why does the speaker call herself a pilgrim? What is a pilgrim?

ART: Draw your IMAGE of what a morning is.

DRAMATIZED INTERVIEW WITH ROBERT FROST (1874–1963)

WAYS TO DRAMATIZE

1. INTRODUCING THE AUTHOR: Give students the interview. Tell students that the interview is based on a letter that Robert Frost wrote to a friend telling why he wrote the poem, *The Road Not Taken.* Read the interview aloud.

2. PAIRS DRAMATIZE: Students act the two roles. Choose two students to dramatize the interview for the class.

3. PERFORMING: Use costume pieces and perform the interview about *The Road Not Taken,* the poem the interview describes, and perhaps other Frost poems.

CAST: (2) TV Announcer, Robert Frost

COSTUME SUGGESTIONS: *Robert Frost:* Checked flannel shirt, shirt unbuttoned at the collar, or other appropriate casual farmer-poet attire; *Woman TV Announcer:* Bright, solid-colored blazer with tasteful blouse and perhaps a scarf; *Male TV Announcer:* Jacket, tie, and spatula or wooden spoon for a microphone

TV Interviewer: Today we meet profound nature poet Robert Frost. Welcome Mr. Frost. We look forward to hearing your profound thoughts on your *very* profound poem, *The Road Not Taken.*

Frost: Thank you. I look forward to giving them.

Interviewer: Now, we are all aware that *The Road Not Taken* is one of *the* most profound American poems.

Frost: Gosh. Thanks a lot.

Interviewer: And hundreds and hundreds of teachers and students have been studying this poem ever since it was printed in 1918.

Frost: That's quite impressive. Since I've been dead since 1963, could you fill me in on some of these lofty interpretations?

Interviewer: Well, some people feel your profound poem is about yourself and the important decision you made in your life not to take a regular 9 to 5 job but to take the "less traveled road" and become a poet. I kind of like that interpretation.

Frost: Uh, huh. And what are some others?

Interviewer: Well, perhaps your profound poem is telling young people that those early decisions they make, such as staying in or dropping out of school, can, as you put it, make "all the difference" in their lives later on.

Frost: Ohh, that *is* heavy!

Interviewer: We, of course, are sitting here at the edge of our seats waiting to hear the *real* interpretation from the poet.

Frost: Are you *sure* you want my interpretation?

Interviewer: Of course, that's why we brought you on the show

Frost: O.K. Well, you see I had this friend who would worry about everything. For example, he worried whether he should go to a party that night or stay home. He worried whether he should buy black or brown socks. He'd worry whether he should talk to a friend on the phone or read a book. And he was always sighing that he might have made the wrong decision.

Interviewer: *(Interrupting.)* Excuse me. But what's that got to do with your profound poem?

Frost: Don't you see this poem is about my friend taking one road in the woods and not another one and worrying and sighing about it for the rest of his life?

Interviewer: Mr. Frost. You know I don't like that interpretation.

Frost: That's O.K. I wouldn't trust me anyhow. Everyone knows you can't ask a poet what his poem means. You've got to let the poem speak for itself. So, my advice to you is to keep on studying my poems and, of course, buying lots of my books. It makes me feel good that you people want to spend all that time on my little poem and that these two little roads here in New England have made such a difference.

THE PASTURE *by Robert Frost (1874–1963)*

ABOUT THE POEM: This is the first poem in a book of a collection of Frost's poems. The poem describes a little incident on the farm.

WAYS TO DRAMATIZE

1. INTRODUCING THE POEM: Copy the poem for students. Discuss About the Poem. Use the interview with Frost and other Frost poems as needed.

2. EVERYBODY DRAMATIZES: Recite the poem using gestures. Then have students recite the poem and gesture with you.

3. PAIRS OR GROUPS DRAMATIZE: Divide the class into two groups. Group One plays the Speaker enticing the Friend to join him. Group Two listens. Reverse the roles. Then, divide the class into pairs to play the Speaker and the Friend. Some may dramatize for the class.

4. PERFORMING: Use costume pieces and perform the poem for others, perhaps with the interview and other Frost poems.

CAST: (2) Speaker, Friend

COSTUME SUGGESTIONS: *Speaker and Friend:* Appropriate farm hats or other farm clothing

INSTRUMENT SUGGESTIONS: Strike a triangle at the end of each verse.

THE PASTURE by Robert Frost

I'm going out to clean the pasture spring;

I'll only stop to rake the leaves away *(Rake leaves.)*

(And wait to watch the water clear, I may):

I sha'n't be gone long. —You come too. *(Beckon with an arm.)*

I'm going out to fetch the little calf *(Pat calf.)*

That's standing by the mother. It's so young

It totters when she licks it with her tongue. *(Totter. Move head as if licking calf.)*

I sha'n't be gone long. — You come too. *(Beckon with an arm.)*

TOPICS FOR CRITICAL THINKING, WRITING, AND ART

1. Some poems are more difficult than others to understand. Would you call this poem easy or difficult to understand? Explain.

2. This poem describes a little incident on a farm. Tell what happens in the poem.

3. What lines in each stanza RHYME?

4. Which lines are repeated. Why?

5. In good poetry, readers need to use their imaginations to fill in the details. For example, who do you think the speaker is talking to when he says, "You come too."

6. Would you call the TONE of this poem—powerful, gentle, mournful, friendly, spooky, or joyous? Recite or underline a line or a phrase to prove your answer.

ART: Draw the little calf.

THE ROAD NOT TAKEN *by Robert Frost* (1874–1963)

ABOUT THIS POEM: A person on a walk in the woods sees two roads and decides to walk up one rather than another.

WAYS TO DRAMATIZE

1. INTRODUCING THE POEM: Copy poem for students. Discuss About the Poem and use the interview with Robert Frost that describes his experience writing this poem.

2. EVERYBODY DRAMATIZES: Recite the poem using good articulation and speaking slowly, and then have students recite it with you.

3. PAIRS OR GROUPS DRAMATIZE: Divide the class into two groups and have each recite every other stanza. Then, divide the class into groups of four to dramatize the poem. Some groups might choose to use several narrators. Some might want to dramatize the two roads. Have some perform for the class.

4. PERFORMING: Use costume pieces and perform the poem for others with the interview and, perhaps other Frost poems or seasonal poems. (See Subject Index Across the Curriculum.)

CAST: Traveler, Trees

COSTUME SUGGESTIONS: *Traveler:* Fall hat and coat; *Trees:* Artificial autumn leaf branches or hold yellow construction paper leaves.

THE ROAD NOT TAKEN by Robert Frost

Two roads diverged* in a yellow wood, *(Raise 2 fingers and arms create 2 roads.)*

*to lie in different directions

And sorry I could not travel both *(Shake head.)*
And be one traveler, long I stood
And looked down one as far as I could *(Shade eyes.)*
To where it bent in the undergrowth; *(Arm makes bent road.)*

Then took the other, as just as fair,
And having perhaps the better claim,
Because it was grassy and wanted wear; *(Fingers make grass.)*
Though as for that, the passing there
Had worn them really about the same, *(Fingers on both hands make grass.)*

And both that morning equally lay *(Arms stretch out making two roads.)*
In leaves no step had trodden black.
Oh, I kept the first for another day! *(Hold up index finger and arm creates first road.)*
Yet knowing how way leads on to way,
I doubted if I should ever come back. *(Shake head.)*

I shall be telling this with a sigh *(Bow head.)*
Somewhere ages and ages hence:
Two roads diverged in a wood, and I— *(Raise two fingers and arms create two roads.)*
I took the one less traveled by, *(Point to self.)*
And that has made all the difference. *(Shake head slowly.)*

TOPICS FOR CRITICAL THINKING, WRITING, AND ART

1. What season of the year is implied when the poem says "two roads diverged in a yellow wood"?

2. A SYMBOL is something that means more than what it is. For example, the roads in the poem are two roads in the woods, but the poem implies that they may also mean something more about ourselves and the decisions we make in life. Explain how a decision in a young man or woman's life might be like choosing one road or over another and "make all the difference."

3. The speaker says taking one road rather than another has "made all the difference." Tell about sometime in your life when you had to choose between two things that seemed equally good or right to do.

4. This poem has an unusual rhyme scheme. Which lines in each stanza rhyme?

5. Frost came from Vermont where there is beautiful fall foliage. Find a picture of Vermont or New England fall foliage and display it in the room.

ART: Illustrate the two roads in the "yellow woods."

THE RUNAWAY *by Robert Frost (1874–1963)*

(Scripted for Dramatization by Louise Thistle)

ABOUT THE POEM: A man and woman stop in the woods in a snowstorm when they see a frightened colt.

WAYS TO DRAMATIZE

1. INTRODUCING THE POEM: Copy poem for students. Discuss About the Poem. Use the interview with Frost and other Frost poems as needed. Recite the poem—using a deeper voice for the man and a lighter one for the woman.

2. EVERYBODY DRAMATIZES: Recite the poem along with the students.

3. PAIRS OR GROUPS DRAMATIZE: Divide the class into pairs to dramatize the poem. The poem is cast with a man and a woman, but students of the same sex may play both roles. Or divide the class into groups to also play Colt, Snow. (The horse might use stylized movements and freeze when not part of the narration.)

4. PERFORMING: Use costume pieces, props, and instruments; perform the poem for others, perhaps with other Frost poems.

CAST: (4) Man, Woman, Colt, Snow (Actor playing Snow might create sound effects.)

COSTUME AND PROP SUGGESTIONS: *Snow:*Dowels with long white crepe paper attached, *Man.* Winter cap or jacket; *Woman:* Scarf and hat

INSTRUMENT SUGGESTIONS: Strike a wood block for the running of the horse; shake jingle bells when he "bolts" and "shudders his coat."

THE RUNAWAY *by Robert Frost*

Woman:
The Runaway

Man:
By Robert Frost

Man:
Once when the snow of the year was beginning to fall, *(Fingers create falling snow.)*
We stopped by a mountain pasture to say, "Whose colt?"
A little Morgan* had one forefoot on the wall, *(Arm creates forefoot.)*
The other curled at his breast. He dipped his head *(Curl other arm by breast. Dip head.)*
And snorted at us. And then he had to bolt. *(Shake head. Snort. Bolt with head.)*
We heard the miniature thunder where he fled, *(Strike desk.)*
And we saw him, or thought we saw him, dim and gray
Like a shadow against the curtain of falling flakes. *(Fingers create flakes.)*

Woman: *(Concerned.)*
"I think the little fellow's afraid of the snow.
He isn't winter-broken. It isn't play
With the little fellow at all. He's running away.
I doubt if even his mother could tell him, 'Sakes, it's only weather,'
He'd think she didn't know!
Where is his mother? He can't be out alone."

Man:
And now he comes again with a clatter of stone, *(Strike wood block.)*
And mounts the wall again with whited eyes *(Show whited eyes.)*
And all his tail that isn't hair up straight.
He shudders his coat as if to throw off flies. *(Shudder.)*

Woman: *(Assertively.)*
"Whoever it is that leaves him out so late,
When other creatures have gone to stall and bin,
Ought to be told to come and take him in."

* Morgan: a breed of horse named for Joseph Morgan

TOPICS FOR CRITICAL THINKING, WRITING, AND ART

1. The poet paints a vivid picture of the colt. Underline all the lines that describe the colt's behavior.

2. Why do you think the woman feels the little fellow is "afraid of the snow"? Show "whited eyes" with your eyes. How does it feel when you show "whited eyes"? What does "whited eyes" mean?

3. "Miniature thunder" is a METAPHOR. What does "miniature thunder" represent?

ART: Illustrate one line of your choice that describes the "little Morgan."

THE ROBIN *by Thomas Hardy (1840–1928)*

ABOUT THE POEM: The speaker imagines himself as a Robin.

WAYS TO DRAMATIZE

1. INTRODUCING THE POEM: Give students a copy of the poem. Discuss About the Poem.

2. EVERYBODY DRAMATIZES: Recite the poem, and then have students recite it with you.

3. PAIRS OR GROUPS DRAMATIZE: Have half of the class narrate while the other half plays the bird doing its actions. Then, divide the class into three groups. In succession, Group One recites the poem doing gestures, then Group Two, and finally Group Three. Last, dramatize the poem in pairs with one narrating and the other acting.

4. PERFORMING: Use costume pieces and instruments to perform the poem for others.

CAST:(2) Narrator, Bird

COSTUME SUGGESTIONS: *Bird:* Brown baseball cap; *Pools:* Blue, filmy fabric

INSTRUMENT SUGGESTIONS: Use jingle bells or a triangle to emphasize the action.

THE ROBIN by Thomas Hardy
abridged and adapted by Louise Thistle

When up aloft* *(Raise arms up.)* * high

in the air

I fly and fly, *(Flap wings.)*

I see in pools (*Look down.*)

The shining sky, *(Arms reach up.)*

And a happy bird *(Flap wings.)*

Am I, Am I! *(Continue flapping.)*

TOPICS FOR CRITICAL THINKING, WRITING, AND ART

1. Who is the speaker in the poem?

2. Is the TONE of the poem—serious, comical, joyful, melancholy? What words are used that prove your answer?

3. What does it mean that the speaker sees "in pools /The shining sky"? What are "the pools"? How is the speaker looking at the sky?

4. Which lines in the poem RHYME? Why does the poet repeat "Am I" at the end of the poem?

5. Why might dancers like this poem?

ART: Study pictures of robins and then draw one.

DRAMATIZED INTERVIEW WITH LANGSTON HUGHES (1902–67)

WAYS TO DRAMATIZE

1. Introducing the Author: Give students the interview. Explain that it's based on Langston Hughes' own words on how he came to write *The Negro Speaks of Rivers.*

2. Pairs Dramatize: In pairs, have students act the two roles. Choose two students to dramatize the interview for the class.

3. Performing: Use costume pieces and props to perform the poem along with other poems by Hughes.

CAST: (2) TV Announcer, Langston Hughes

COSTUME SUGGESTIONS: *Langston Hughes:* Suit jacket and tie; *Woman TV Announcer; Male TV Announcer:* Jacket, tie; *Microphone:* Spatula or wooden spoon

TV Interviewer: Mr. Hughes, you've said you wrote, *The Negro Speaks of Rivers,* when you were on a train crossing the Mississippi River.

Hughes: Yes, the train was going over a long bridge at sunset. I looked out the window at the great muddy Mississippi flowing down toward the heart of the South.

TV Interviewer: And you began to think what that river meant to African-Americans in the past.

Hughes: Yes, "to be sold down the river" was the worst fate that could happen to a slave in times of slavery. Then, I thought about other rivers in our Black history—the Congo, the Niger, and the Nile in Africa. And the thought came to me: "I've known rivers," and I put it down on the back of an envelope.

TV Interviewer: How long did it take you to write the poem?

Hughes: Within ten to fifteen minutes, as the train gathered speed in the dusk, I had written the poem, which I called, *The Negro Speaks of Rivers.*

TV Interviewer: That is remarkable. It's a powerful poem and exciting to dramatize. There's a kind of hypnotic rhythm in it.

Hughes: I think that Jazz is one of the inherent expressions of Negro life in America. It's the eternal drum beating in the Negro soul, and I tried to get that energy in the poem.

TV Interviewer: Well, you certainly did, and I bet students will enjoy dramatizing it.

DREAMS *by Langston Hughes (1902–67)*

ABOUT THE POEM: A parent advises his son to hold a dream in his heart and keep it.

WAYS TO DRAMATIZE

1. INTRODUCING THE POEM: Give students a copy of the poem. Discuss About the Poem.

2. EVERYBODY DRAMATIZES: Recite each line of the poem using good articulation and speaking slowly. Then have students say the line with you. Next, recite the poem with students using gestures.

3. PAIRS OR GROUPS DRAMATIZE: Divide the class into two groups. Group one recites Speaker One's lines and Group Two, Speaker Two's. Then, divide the class into groups of four to dramatize the poem. Some groups may dramatize it for the class.

4. PERFORMING: Use costume pieces and instruments. Perform the poem for others perhaps including the interview and other poems by Hughes.

CAST: (4) Narrator-parent, Bird, Snow (2)

SUGGESTED COSTUME PIECES: *Bird:* Black baseball cap; *Snow:* White strip of cloth held taut by the two actors.

SUGGESTED INSTRUMENTS: Use a triangle, wood block, and rattle as indicated on the script to accent the action.

DREAMS by Langston Hughes

Speaker One:
Dreams

Speaker Two:
By Langston Hughes

Speaker One:
Hold fast to dreams, my son, *(Hands on heart.)*
Hold fast to dreams, O boy,
Hold fast to dreams.
Strike triangle.
For if dreams die *(Hands and head bend down.)*
Strike wood block.
Life is a broken-winged bird *(Arm makes broken wing.)*
Shake rattle.
That cannot fly. *(Shake head slowly.)*
Shake rattle.

Speaker Two:
Hold fast to dreams. *(Hands on heart.)*
Strike triangle.
For when dreams go *(Push arms away from body.)*
Strike wood block.
Life is a barren* field *(Arms stretch out creating field.)*
Shake rattle.
Frozen with snow. *(Freeze, hold hands up rigidly.)*
Shake rattle.

* barren: not capable of producing or growing anything.

TOPICS FOR CRITICAL THINKING, WRITING, AND ART

1. The poem is called *Dreams.* What kind of dreams is it talking about?

2. The poet uses a METAPHOR comparing a life without dreams to "a barren field frozen with snow." What is the feeling someone might have standing in "a barren field frozen with snow"? How is a life without dreams "a barren field frozen with snow"? What in nature might be a METAPHOR of a young life full of possibilities and dreams?

3. The speaker addresses the poem to "my son." Who do you think is speaking to the son? How old do you think the son is? Why do you think the speaker is giving the son this advice now?

4. In what way are the speakers in *Mother to Son* and *Dreams* giving the son the same advice? Would they give the same kind of advice to a daughter? Explain.

ART: Depict some dream you have for your life.

MOTHER TO SON *by Langston Hughes* (1902–67)

ABOUT THE POEM: A mother tells her son to keep striving and to not "give up" or "give in."

WAYS TO DRAMATIZE

1. INTRODUCING THE POEM: Give students a copy of the poem. Discuss About the Poem. Compare the poem to *Dreams,* another Hughes poem in this book. Recite the poem using good articulation and speaking slowly.

2. EVERYBODY DRAMATIZES: Recite each line of the poem. Then have students recite each line with you.

3. GROUPS OR PAIRS DRAMATIZE: Choose ten students to play Mothers (or Fathers) and have them recite their assigned lines. Then, dramatize the poem in pairs using a Mother and Son or Father and Son. ("Son" could be changed to "Daughter.")

4. PERFORMING: Stage the poem with the Mother or Father sitting facing their child and the audience while the Son or Daughter sits with his or her back to the audience.

CAST (2) Mother and Son or Daughter, or Father and Son or Daughter

COSTUME SUGGESTIONS: *Mother:* Apron; *Son or daughter:* Baseball cap or other appropriate teen attire

MOTHER TO SON by Langston Hughes

Mother or Father 1:

Well, son, I'll tell you:

#2: Life for me ain't been no crystal stair. *(Shake head.)*

#3: It's had tacks in it, *(Fingers show tacks.)*

#4 And splinters, *(Fingers show splinters.)*

#5: And boards torn up,

#6: And places with no carpet on the floor—

#7: Bare. *(Push hands to sides showing "bare.")*

#8: But all the time

#9: I'se been a-climbin' on, *(Mime climbing.)*

#10 And reachin' landin's, *(Pause.)*

#1: And turnin' corners,

#2: And sometimes goin' in the dark *(Squint.)*

#3: Where there ain't been no light.

#4: So boy, don't you turn back.

#5: Don't you set down on the steps *(Gesture toward steps.)*

#6: 'Cause you finds it's kinder hard.

#7: Don't you fall now— *(Gesture to ground on "fall.")*

#8: For I'se still goin', honey, *(Move body as if climbing.)*

#9: I'se still climbin', *(Hands climb.)*

#10: And life for me ain't been no crystal stair. *(Shake head, then nod.)*

TOPICS FOR CRITICAL THINKING, WRITING, AND ART

1. Why does the poet use words such as *goin'* and *climbin'* instead of *going* and *climbing* as well as expressions such as, "There ain't been no light" instead of "There hasn't been any light," which is standard English speech? What is gained by this use of language in this poem?

2. Somebody said the most important quality parents can instill in their children is persistence. What is persistence? Why do you think the mother is telling the son to persist? What is the opposite of persistence? Why in the situation of this mother and son does it take even more courage and character to persist? What might happen to the son if he doesn't persist?

3. The first seven lines of the poem describe the Mother's experience of life as harsh unpleasant objects. What are four harsh objects she mentions? The remainder of the poem uses active verbs or phrases to describe her struggles. List or underline these phrases.

ART: Illustrate your image of a crystal stair or draw the mother's description of her real life dilapidated stairs. Write the line that describes your stairs on your paper.

THE NEGRO SPEAKS OF RIVERS
by Langston Hughes (1902–67)

ABOUT THE POEM: The poem traces the African-American's connection with rivers worldwide. It shows how through the memory of this connection that the African-American's soul has become "deep like the rivers." (The earliest man known was in Africa. The "dawn" to which Hughes refers is the Tigris and Euphrates River area where supposedly Western Civilization began.)

WAYS TO DRAMATIZE

1. Introducing the Poem: Give students a copy of the poem. Discuss About the Poem. Use the interview with Langston Hughes describing how he wrote *The Negro Speaks of Rivers.* Locate the rivers mentioned in the poem on a map. Recite the poem speaking slowly.

2. Everybody Dramatizes: Recite the poem divided into manageable sections that students then repeat with you.

3. Groups or Pairs Dramatize: Cast the poem with eight Narrators. The class plays the Chorus. Then, divide students into groups to dramatize the poem. Some groups could perform it for the class.

4. Performing: Use costume pieces and perform the poem for others using the interview and perhaps other Hughes poems.

CAST: (11 or fewer) Speakers: Use 8 Speakers (or as many as desired), Rivers (2 or more), Sunset

COSTUME SUGGESTIONS: *Rivers*: Use filmy blue, dusky brown, or beige filmy fabric for the different rivers. *Sun:* Use a large cardboard sun covered with gold or orange foil.

INSTRUMENT SUGGESTIONS: Use a background drum beat throughout the poem or at the end of lines to accentuate the rhythm.

THE NEGRO SPEAKS OF RIVERS by Langston Hughes

Speaker 1:

The Negro Speaks of Rivers
By Langston Hughes

Chorus:

I've known rivers:

Speaker 1:

I've known rivers ancient as the world

Speaker 2:

and older than the
flow of human blood in human veins.

Chorus:

My soul has grown deep like the rivers.

Speaker 3:

I bathed in the Euphrates* when dawns were young. * A river and valley in Egypt where civilization began

Speaker 4:

I built my hut near the Congo and it lulled me to sleep.

Speaker 5:

I looked upon the Nile and raised the pyramids above it.

Speaker 6:

I heard the singing of the Mississippi when Abe Lincoln
went down to New Orleans,

Speaker 7:

and I've seen its muddy
bosom turn all golden in the sunset.

Speaker 8:

I've known rivers:
Ancient, dusky* rivers. *dark

Chorus:

My soul has grown deep like the rivers. *(Chant twice, slow the pace the second time.)*

TOPICS FOR CRITICAL THINKING, WRITING, AND ART

1. In the interview, using the poet's own words, Hughes says that he wrote *The Negro Speaks of Rivers* in ten to fifteen minutes. How do you think he could write such a powerful poem in so short a time?

2. The poem creates a RHYTHM by repetition. Find all the lines with the word *rivers* in them. Recite them. Many other lines begin with *I* followed by an active verb. Recite these lines and experience the rhythm.

3. Often in writing, we are told not to use the word *I* frequently and to keep ourselves in the background. Why is it important in this poem for the speaker to use *I*? Who is the speaker speaking for?

ART: Draw a picture of your IMAGE of one of the rivers in the poem.

DRAMATIZED INTERVIEW WITH CHRISTINA ROSSETTI (1830–1894)

WAYS TO DRAMATIZE

1. INTRODUCING THE AUTHOR: Give students the interview. Read the interview aloud—using a bright energetic voice for the Announcer and a mellow steady voice for Rossetti. Then, ask students why Christina Rossetti's chose to go on the *Meet the Poets* show?

2. PAIRS DRAMATIZE: In pairs, students act the two roles. Choose two students to dramatize the roles for the class.

3. PERFORMING: Use costume pieces and perform the interview with other Rossetti poems.

CAST: *(2)* TV Announcer (animated); Christina Rossetti (dedicated to poetry and a religious view of life)

COSTUME AND PROP SUGGESTIONS: *Christina Rossetti:* Lace or chiffon scarf or fabric to cover the head, large cross on a chain; *Woman TV Announcer:* Bright, solid-colored blazer with tasteful blouse and perhaps a scarf. *Male TV Announcer:* Jacket, tie. *Microphone:* Use kitchen whisk, wooden spoon, or any object with a handle and a round end.

DRAMATIZED INTERVIEW WITH CHRISTINA ROSSETTI

TV Announcer: Today we are fortunate to have in the studio the famous nature and religious poet, Christina Rossetti. Miss Rossetti, we know you're shy so it's an honor that you've agreed to appear on the *Meet the Poets* show.

Christina: I believe the Lord wished me to come before you to talk about poetry and the religious way of life.

TV Announcer: I see, very interesting. Now you lived in London from 1830 to 1894. Anything exciting going on then?

Christina: It was the time of pre-Raphaelite art. We believed in carefully following nature. My brother, Daniel, was a famous painter and poet then too. His paintings are popular today.

TV Announcer: And he encouraged you.

Christina: I owe first credit to my dear grandfather. He spent his own money to have my first poems published privately when I was seventeen years old.

TV Announcer: Kind of like self-publishing.

Christina: Yes, but only a few people saw my poems until my brother Daniel helped me get them printed for the public when I was thirty-two.

TV Announcer: You are very good looking, in fact, beautiful as your brother has said. Many of your poems are beautiful and sensitive too. Why do you dress drably?

Christina: My brother always said that too, but I don't feel the Lord wants me to dress richly. He wants me to dedicate my life, I believe, to poetry and to helping others.

TV Announcer: I also heard that you were in love with a man who wanted to marry you, but you refused. Why?

Christina: He was not dedicated enough to my religious way of life.

TV Announcer: We're now going to perform some of your poems. Would you like to tell us what they mean?

Christina: I believe in letting the poems speak for themselves. If the spirit of the Lord is in them, then the meaning will be clear.

TV Announcer: Thank you Christina for appearing on *Meet the Poets.* I know you are intensely shy, but I'm sure our audience very much enjoyed seeing you and hearing your thoughts. Now, we'll let your poems speak for themselves.

CATERPILLAR *by Christina Rossetti* (1830–1894)

ABOUT THE POEM: The speaker, seeing a caterpillar hurrying down the walk, hopes it will someday become a butterfly.

WAYS TO DRAMATIZE

1. INTRODUCING THE POEM: Give students a copy of the poem. Discuss About the Poem, above.

2. EVERYBODY DRAMATIZES: Recite each couplet, speaking as if addressing the caterpillar. Students repeat the couplet with the teacher. Then, recite the whole poem with students slowly adding gestures.

3. PAIRS OR GROUPS DRAMATIZE: Have students suggest and demonstrate to the class how they might dramatize each couplet. Using students' suggestions, cast the roles and dramatize the poem for the class. Then, divide the class into groups to dramatize the poem. Some may dramatize it for the class.

4. PERFORMING: Use costume pieces and perform the poem for others perhaps with the interview and other Rossetti poems.

CAST: (3 to 6) Narrator, Caterpillar, Leaf, Stalk, Toad, and Bird (An actor may play more than one part.)

COSTUME SUGGESTIONS: *Caterpillar:* Brown furry hat; *Leaf and Stalk:* Green material over shoulders; *Frog:* Green baseball cap turned backwards with large eyes attached; *Bird:* yellow baseball cap; *Butterfly:* white nylon netting draped around body for cocoon and orange or yellow netting over shoulders as newborn butterfly

INSTRUMENT SUGGESTIONS: Use a wood block, rattles, a guiro, and a triangle to accent the action.

CATERPILLAR by Christina Rossetti

Brown and furry

Caterpillar in a hurry, (*Wiggle like a caterpillar.*)

Scrape guiro.

Take your walk *(Do "wiggle" walk,* stop.)

Tap wood block lightly.

To the shady leaf, or stalk, *(Arms create leaf and then a stalk.)*

Strike triangle.

Or what not, *(Shrug.)*

Which may be the chosen spot. *(Point at a spot.)*

Strike triangle.

No toad spy you, *(Squat.)*

Strike wood block.

Hovering bird of prey pass by you; *(Arms make wings.)*

Shake jingle bells.

Spin and die, *(Spin arm. Slump over.)*

Scrape guiro.

To live again a butterfly. *(Spread wings, flutter, freeze.)*

Strike triangle rapidly several times.

TOPICS FOR CRITICAL THINKING, WRITING, AND ART

1. *Caterpillar* is written in COUPLETS (meaning every *couple* or pair of lines rhyme. Which words rhyme in each COUPLET?

2. The poet watches the caterpillar. She also empathizes or "feels for" it. What does the speaker say that shows she "feels" protective toward the caterpillar? Why do you think she feels so strongly about it?

3 The poem is about a caterpillar who will hopefully become a butterfly. In what way might the poem also be a SYMBOL (meaning something more than just a caterpillar) and be also about what adults hope will happen in the life of a young person?

ART: In the poem a caterpillar hopefully will transform into a butterfly. What other things in nature and in life transform from one thing to another? Draw a picture of the transformation.

UPHILL *by Christina Rossetti (1830–1894)*

ABOUT THE POEM: A young person is about to take a journey and asks someone who's taken the journey before for advice. The poem is scripted for dramatization.

WAYS TO DRAMATIZE

1. INTRODUCING THE POEM: Give students a copy of the poem. Discuss About the Poem.

2. EVERYBODY DRAMATIZES: Recite each line of the poem focusing on good articulation. Have students repeat each line with you.

3. PAIRS OR GROUPS DRAMATIZE: Divide the class into two groups. Group One plays the Young Traveler and Group Two, the Older Traveler. Lead the two groups as they recite. Reverse the roles. Then, choose two students—one with a more mature deep voice and the other with higher lighter voice to perform the Young and Old Traveler. Finally, divide the students into pairs to dramatize the poem. Emphasize using a higher, younger, questioning voice for the Young Traveler and a stronger, deeper, mature voice for the Older Traveler. Some might dramatize for the class. Perhaps use costume pieces.

4. PERFORMING: Use costume pieces and perform the poem for others with the interview and perhaps other Rossetti poems.

CAST: (2) Young Traveler, Older Traveler

SUGGESTED COSTUME PIECES: *Young Traveler:* Baseball cap or other young-style hat; *Older Traveler:* Derby or mature female hat, business jacket or other mature clothing.

UPHILL by Christina Rossetti

Young Traveler:

Does the road wind uphill all the way?

Older Traveler:

Yes, to the very end.

Young Traveler:

Will the day's journey take the whole long day?

Older Traveler:

From morn to night, my friend.

Young Traveler:

But is there for the night a resting-place?
A roof for when the slow dark hours begin.
May not the darkness hide it from my face?

Older Traveler:

You cannot miss that inn.

Young Traveler:

Shall I meet other wayfarers* at night?
Those who have gone before.
Then must I knock, or call when just in sight?

Older Traveler:

They will not keep you standing at that door.

* foot travelers

Young Traveler:

Shall I find comfort, travel-sore and weak?

Old Traveler:

Of labor you shall find the sum.

Young Traveler:

Will there be beds for me and all who seek?

Old Traveler:

Yea, beds for all who come.

TOPICS FOR CRITICAL THINKING, WRITING, AND ART

1. The poem describes a journey a young person might take. In what way might this journey also be a SYMBOL meaning something more, such as other new undertakings in life, like leaving elementary school for middle school or high school for college. Describe a time when you had to try something new or go into a new situation and you felt uncertain and anxious as the Young Traveler does.

2. What makes the journey difficult? How can a person find comfort during the journey?

3. In Pairs, pretend that one of you is a kindergarten teacher and the other a frightened child on his first day of school. What might the child say to show he is scared? What might the teacher say to comfort him? Practice your dramatization. Some groups could enact them for the class.

4. The poem is divided into four STANZAS. (A STANZA is a unit of thought similar to a paragraph and marked off by white space.) Tell what each new worry or concern the young traveler has in each stanza.

5. This poem follows a RHYME SCHEME called a-b-a-b, meaning that the first and third lines and the second and fourth lines rhyme. Tell which words rhyme in each of the stanzas and mark the rhyming words.

ART: Draw a scene with a road going up a hill. Place something in the picture that might be of comfort to a weary traveler.

*For another dramatized Rossetti poem, *The Wind,* see the performance script pages 226–227.

FOG *by Carl Sandburg (1878–1967)*

ABOUT THE POEM: The movement of the fog is compared to a quiet cat entering and leaving a city.

WAYS TO DRAMATIZE

1. INTRODUCING THE POEM: Give students a copy of the poem. Discuss About the Poem. Tell students to listen how the poem describes fog in an unusual way. Recite the poem slowly with good articulation to create a mysterious mood.

2. EVERYBODY DRAMATIZES: Recite each line again with students reciting with you. Discuss each line. Then recite the whole poem with students adding gestures.

3. PAIRS OR GROUPS DRAMATIZE: Choose six students to recite and dramatize each line. Then, divide the students into pairs or groups to dramatize the poem. Some groups could dramatize it for the class.

4. PERFORMING: Use costume pieces and instruments to perform the poem for others, perhaps with other seasonal or weather poems. (See Subject Index Across the Curriculum.)

CAST: (2 or more) Narrator, Fog that transforms into cat. (Perhaps use one or two as Fog and several Cats.)

COSTUME SUGGESTIONS: *Fog* and *Cat:* Hold up white nylon netting and creep behind it.

INSTRUMENT SUGGESTIONS: Wood block, rattles.

FOG by Carl Sandburg

The fog comes *(Arms make fog.)*

Shake rattle lightly.

on little cat feet. *(Walk "in place" like a cat.)*

Tap wood block lightly.

It sits looking *(Crouch. Look around.)*

Shake rattle lightly.

over harbor and city *(Stretch neck forward.)*

on silent haunches* *(Hunch shoulders down.)*

and then moves on. *(Continue cat walk.)*

Tap wood block lightly.

* hips

TOPICS FOR CRITICAL THINKING, WRITING, AND ART

1. Sandburg compares the coming and going of the fog (using a METAPHOR) to the quiet movement of a cat. PANTOMIME the quiet movement of a cat. In what ways might a fog's movement be like that of a cat?

2. There is something mysterious and unpredictable about fog. Cats are mysterious and unpredictable. Give an example of the unpredictable or mysterious behavior of a cat and how a cat might come and go like fog.

3. Why might dancers like this poem?

ART: Draw the cat described in the poem or draw the harbor and city in the fog.

DRAMATIZED INTERVIEW WITH WILLIAM SHAKESPEARE
(1564–1616)

WAYS TO DRAMATIZE

1. INTRODUCING THE AUTHOR: Give students the interview. Read the interview—changing your voice to distinguish the two characters. Model good articulation. Then, ask what speaking skills Shakespeare wants actors to use.

2. PAIRS DRAMATIZE: In pairs, students act the two roles. Choose two students to dramatize the roles for the class.

3. PERFORMING: Use costume pieces and perform the interview with other Shakespeare poems.

CAST:(2) TV Announcer (very animated); Shakespeare (perky, confident, and obsessed with the importance of good speaking and acting skills)

SUGGESTED COSTUME PIECES AND PROPS: *Shakespeare:* A Renaissance style hat with a flamboyant feather; *Woman TV Announcer:* Bright, solid-colored blazer with tasteful blouse and perhaps a scarf. *Male TV Announcer:* Jacket, tie. *Microphone:* Use kitchen whisk, wooden spoon or any object with a handle and a round end.

TV Announcer: His name is William Shakespeare. He lived in the Renaissance, exciting times. He wrote excellent sonnets and exceptional plays.

Shakespeare: I was also an excellent actor.

TV Announcer: But you are known for your plays.

Shakespeare: One reason why I wrote great plays was because I was an actor. I knew from acting what would work on the stage.

TV Announcer: And you were greatly talented.

Shakespeare: Yes, in fact, a genius. Many people think I am and will always be the GREATEST writer who ever lived.

TV Announcer: That's quite an achievement.

Shakespeare: Of course, it also was hard, hard work—getting the ideas, writing the script, reworking it in rehearsals and rewriting it.

TV Announcer: Rewriting it! I thought geniuses never made a mistake or "blotted a line" as they used to say.

Shakespeare: As you perform a play, you see things that don't play well. The actors moving around speaking the lines tell you instantly whether the dialogue works.

TV Announcer: Well, all your effort was worth it. Now, do you have one piece of advice that you'd like to give these players as they are about to act some of your pieces?

Shakespeare: Yes, to quote myself from my most famous play, *Hamlet*, "Speak the speech I pray you as I pronounced it to you, trippingly on the tongue."

TV Announcer: What is "trippingly on the tongue"?

Shakespeare: Use good *articulation.* "But if you mouth it as many of your players do, I had as lief the town crier spoke my words..."

TV Announcer: What, is "mouth it..."?

Shakespeare: That means yell it out like the old town criers did when they made announcements to the city without any feeling for the sound or meaning of the words.

TV Announcer: Very interesting. Now, it's about time for us to go to a commercial.

Shakespeare: And another thing, "Nor, do not saw the air too much with your hand, thus." That means don't make excessive gestures.

TV Announcer: Thank you, now we're out of time.

Shakespeare: And my most important advice is "Suit the action to the word, the word to the action." That means to make your gestures and actions go with the meaning of the words.

TV Announcer: Uh, huh. Hey, Harry, cut to the commercial. *(To audience.)* Boy these old-time authors are wordy. Haven't they heard of sound bites?

DOUBLE, DOUBLE TOIL AND TROUBLE
by William Shakespeare (1564–1616)

(From three Witches' speech, Act 4, Scene 1, *Macbeth*)

ABOUT THE POEM: The witches stir up a broth to create trouble and to urge Macbeth to commit greater and greater evil deeds.

WAYS TO DRAMATIZE

1. INTRODUCING THE POEM: Give students the selection. Discuss About the Poem and the interview with Shakespeare as needed. Recite the poem using good articulation and projection. Mention that you will not use a "croaking" witch voice that irritates the throat and grates an audience.

2. EVERYBODY DRAMATIZES: Recite each line of the poem and have students recite it with you. Discuss unknown words. Recite the whole poem with students adding gestures.

3. DRAMATIZING IN PAIRS OR GROUPS: Cast four to play each role. Use costume pieces. (The class plays the Chorus chanting the Chorus lines with the actors.) Repeat this with several groups playing the witches. Then, divide the class into groups to dramatize the poem. Some groups could dramatize it for the class.

4. PERFORMING: Use costume pieces to perform the poem for others perhaps with the interview and other selections from Shakespeare.

CAST: (4) Four Witches or Warlocks (male witches)

COSTUME SUGGESTIONS: *Witches or Warlocks*: Black clothing, dark gloves, or perhaps strips of black or raggedy material draped around shoulders and over head.

DOUBLE, DOUBLE TOIL AND TROUBLE
by William Shakespeare

Witch 1:
Double, Double Toil and Trouble

Witch 2:
By William Shakespeare

Class Chorus:
Double, double toil and trouble; *(Stir pot.)*
Fire burn, and cauldron bubble. *(Wiggle fingers.)*

Witch 1:
Fillet* of a fenny* snake *(Hold up snake and shake it.)* *slice *from a swamp
In the cauldron boil and bake. *(Toss snake in. Stir.)*

Witch 2:
Eye of newt* and toe of frog, *(Point to eye, then toe.)* *a salamander
Wool of bat and tongue of dog, *(Spread wings. Stick out tongue.)*

Witch 3:
Adder's fork* and blindworm's* sting, *(Thrust fingers forward twice.)*
*snake's forked tongue *a legless lizard
Lizard's leg and howlet's* wing, *(Point to leg. Spread wings.)* *small owl

Witch 4:
For a charm of powerful trouble, *(Wiggle fingers.)*
Like a hell-broth boil and bubble. *(Stir.)*

Class Chorus:
Double, double toil and trouble; *(Repeat first stanza.)*
Fire burn, and cauldron bubble.

TOPICS FOR CRITICAL THINKING, WRITING, AND ART

1. In the interview, Shakespeare says actors need to practice good ARTICULATION or the speaking of all the syllables in words clearly. Read the witches' speech and tell why this poem needs particularly good articulation.

2. Why do the witches stir these kinds of ingredients in their broth? Why wouldn't it be appropriate to simply add carrots, onions, and salt and pepper? What other ingredients might they add to the evil brew?

3. The witches' incantation is in rhymed couplets (meaning each stanza has a "couple" or two lines and the last word in the two lines rhyme). Tell what words rhyme in each couplet.

4. The sounds of the words Shakespeare uses create a mood helping the witches to cast their evil spell. For example, the repeated *b* and *t* sounds of "Double, double toil and trouble" have an explosive quality when chanted. Recite the "Double, double toil and trouble…" Recite the chorus and experience the explosive *b's* on your lips.

5. ALLITERATION is the repetition of the same consonant sound in words close together. Say "fillet of a fenny snake," "lizard's leg," "boil and bubble."

ART: Draw the cauldron with the witches gathered around creating their evil stew.

WINTER *by William Shakespeare (1564–1616)*

(Song from *Love's Labour's Lost,* Act 5, Scene 2, adapted by Louise Thistle)

ABOUT THE POEM: This song at the end of Shakespeare's play *Love's Labour's Lost* is a singing dialogue between Spring and Winter. Spring is represented by the cuckoo bird and Winter by the owl. (The poem here has been adapted, assigning roles for each line.)

WAYS TO DRAMATIZE

1. INTRODUCING THE POEM: Give students a copy of the poem. Discuss About the Poem and the interview with Shakespeare as needed. Recite the poem.

2. EVERYBODY DRAMATIZES: Slowly recite each line of the poem with students focusing on good articulation. Discuss the images and unknown words. Recite the whole poem slowly with students adding gestures.

3. DRAMATIZING IN PAIRS OR GROUPS: Cast individuals to play each role using the cast list. Perhaps, use two narrators with each reciting every other line, or the actors in each line might memorize their line and act it too. Add simple costume pieces and instruments to accentuate the action.

4. PERFORMING: Use costume pieces and instruments to perform the poem for others. Also use the interview and perhaps other Shakespeare poems.

CAST: Icicles, Dick, Servant with Pail, Owl, Joan, Wind, Parishioner, 2 Birds, Marian, Roasted Crabs.

COSTUME AND PROP SUGGESTIONS: *Icicles:* Silver tinsel attached to a card or stick; *Dick:* Knit cap; *Servant:* Pail; *Owl*: Feathered hat or feathers on paper-bag hat or brown, knit hat; *Joan:* Long shawl and wooden spoon; *Wind*: Black cloth or strips of cloth; *Parishioner:* Knit cap of different color than Dick's; *Birds*: Yellow baseball cap; *Marian*: Red kerchief; *Crab apples:* Red gloves

INSTRUMENT SUGGESTIONS: Use jingle bells, wood blocks, rattles, and a guiro to accentuate the language and action.

WINTER by William Shakespeare
adapted by Louise Thistle

Owl:

Winter

By William Shakespeare

Icicles:

When icicles hang by the wall, *(Fingers become icicles.)*

Dick:

And Dick the shepherd blows his nail,* *(Blow fingernails.)* *fingernails

Servant:

And milk comes frozen home in pail, *(Grip handles of frozen pails.)*

All:

When blood is nipped and ways be foul, *(Shiver.)*

Owl:

Then nightly sings the staring owl, *(Stare.)*

"To-who! *(In mysterious singing voice.)*

Tu-whit, tu-who!" a merry note,

Joan:

While greasy Joan doth keel* the pot. *(Stir stew in big pot.)* *to cool by stirring

Wind:

When all aloud the wind doth blow, *(Lean forward—say "SHHHHH!")*

Parishioner:

And coughing drowns the parson's saw,* *(Cough once on "coughing.")*

*droning sermon

Two Birds:

And birds sit brooding in the snow, *(Shake head.)*

Marian:

And Marian's nose looks red and raw, *(Hold cold nose.)*

Roasted Crabs:

When roasted crabs* hiss in the bowl, *(Wiggle fingers.)* *crab apples

Owl:

Then nightly sings the staring owl: *(Stare.)*

"To-who! *(In mysterious singing voice.)*

Tu-whit, tu-who!" a merry note,

Joan:

While greasy Joan doth keel the pot. *(Stir stew in big pot.)*

TOPICS FOR CRITICAL THINKING, WRITING, AND ART

1. Shakespeare is a master of language. Every word in this song "counts" or contributes to painting a picture of cold winter helping you experience the scene yourself. Which lines in the poem can you visualize and experience best?

2. IMAGES (or word pictures) appeal to the five senses of seeing, hearing, smelling, touching, and tasting. Read each line. Name one or more of the five senses for each line.

3. What are two of the coldest IMAGES you can find in the poem?

4. Why is Joan "greasy"? Is it from something she "keels" in the pot or for another reason?

5. Which words in the poem have a meaning different than they do today?

6. Show through PANTOMIME what some of the characters are doing and see if the class can guess which line is being pantomimed.

7. Shakespeare depicts a winter scene in this song. Think of a winter scene that you've experienced. Describe what was in the scene or what people were doing or wearing so we can see the scene in our mind's eye.

ART: Choose one of your favorite lines in the poem to illustrate. Write the line on your picture.

THE EAGLE *by Alfred Lord Tennyson* (1809–92)

ABOUT THE POEM: The reader experiences the power, grandeur, and independent spirit of the eagle.

WAYS TO DRAMATIZE

1. INTRODUCING THE POEM: Give students a copy of the poem. Discuss About the Poem. Show pictures of eagles and discuss their attributes.

2. EVERYBODY DRAMATIZES: Recite each line of the poem using good articulation and speaking slowly. Then have students recite each line with you. Discuss the images and unknown words. Recite the whole poem slowly with students adding gestures.

3. DRAMATIZING IN PAIRS OR GROUPS: Cast a group of students to act and create sound effects. "Block" the poem—placing the Eagle in the center, the sun on a chair behind it, the crag on one side, and the sea on the other side of the stage

4. PERFORMING: Using costume pieces and instruments, perform the poem for others perhaps with *The Robin* by Thomas Hardy, page 119.

CAST: Narrator, Eagle, Crag, Sun, Sea (2)

COSTUME SUGGESTIONS: *Eagle:* Black baseball cap (perhaps with large construction paper eyes); *Sun:* Gold filmy fabric tied around the head; *Azure World:* Blue nylon netting; *Sea:* Deep aqua, silky material.

INSTRUMENT SUGGESTIONS: Triangle, wood block, guiro, tambourine, drum

THE EAGLE by Alfred Lord Tennyson

The Eagle
Strike triangle.

By Alfred Lord Tennyson
Strike triangle.

He clasps the crag* with crooked hands; *(Hands become claws.)* * steep rugged rock
Strike wood block twice.

Close to the sun in lonely lands, *(Arms make sun over head.)*
Shake tambourine lightly.

Ringed with the azure world, he stands. *(Lower arms in wide sweeping motion.)*
Strike triangle three times.

The wrinkled sea beneath him crawls; *(Ripple hands like moving waves.)*
Scrape guiro.

He watches from his mountain walls, *(Stretch wings back ready to fly.)*
Shake tambourine.

And like a thunderbolt he falls. *(Sweep arms dramatically downwards.)*
Strike drum. Strike triangle to end the scene.

TOPICS FOR CRITICAL THINKING, WRITING, AND ART

1. Tennyson uses a RHYME SCHEME in which every word in each stanza rhymes. What are the rhyming words in each stanza?

2. Tennyson uses PERSONIFICATION when he says the eagle has "crooked hands." How might an eagle appear to have "crooked hands"? Show the eagle's crooked hands with your own hands. The poet uses another PERSONIFICATION (giving something inanimate human feelings) when he says the eagle is in "lonely lands." In what way might lands seem lonely?

3. The poem uses HYPERBOLE or exaggeration when it says the Eagle is "close to the sun," which is, of course, billions of miles away. Why might the eagle appear to be "close to the sun"?

4. Tennyson uses a METAPHOR when he calls the sea "wrinkled." Cloth can be wrinkled, but how might the sea appear to be wrinkled?

5. The poem uses the musical device of ALLITERATION—repeating similar consonant sound in words close together. Find the ALLITERATION in lines one and two.

6. Tennyson uses action verbs to describe the activity of the eagle. Mark or say the four action words that describe what the eagle does in the poem.

7. This poem is like a tiny scene. What is the eagle doing in the beginning, middle, and ending of the scene?

8. "Azure world" is a METAPHOR. What is the author talking about when he says that the eagle is "ringed by the azure world"? What is the "azure world"?

9. This poem is appreciated by people of all ages and appears in many books. Why do you think people like it?

10. The eagle is the national bird of the United States. It is also on the Mexican flag and is an important SYMBOL of courage and grandeur for Native Americans. Why do you think so many cultures admire and respect the eagle?

11. Draw a picture illustrating a line of the poem and write the line on the picture. Or write the whole poem and make an illustration to go with it.

12. Why is this a good poem to dramatize?

13. Tennyson uses a SIMILE in line 6 when he says, "like a thunderbolt, he [the eagle] falls." In what way is the eagle like a thunderbolt?

14. What do readers mean when then they say that *The Eagle* helps them imaginatively participate in the experience of the eagle?

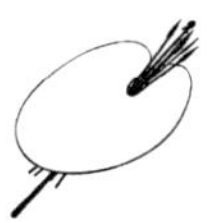

ART: Draw an eagle as depicted in one line of the poem and write that line on your paper. Or draw your own symbol of an eagle as those on a quarter, a dollar bill, poster, or other advertising.

O CAPTAIN! MY CAPTAIN! *by Walt Whitman* (1819–92)

ABOUT THE POEM: Abraham Lincoln is arguably America's greatest President. He saved the country—ending the war that divided the North and South and abolishing slavery. Just as he accomplished these great deeds and the people rejoiced with him, Lincoln was shot by a fanatic while watching a play in a theater.

WAYS TO DRAMATIZE

1. INTRODUCING THE POEM: Give students a copy of the poem. Discuss About the Poem. Discuss the metaphor comparing the Captain to the president of the United States and the ship to the nation.

2. EVERYBODY DRAMATIZES: Recite each line of the poem. Then, have students recite the line with you. Discuss the images and unknown words.

3. DRAMATIZING IN PAIRS OR GROUPS: Cast seven students to recite the seven Speaker roles. The rest of the class plays the Chorus. Then, divide students into groups to dramatize the poem. Some groups could dramatize it for the class.

4. PERFORMING: Use costume pieces and instruments to perform the poem for others.

CAST: (7) Speakers

COSTUME SUGGESTIONS: *Speakers*: Tunics or all-black clothing.

INSTRUMENT SUGGESTIONS: Ring a ship's bell or strike low piano notes at the end of each verse.

O CAPTAIN! MY CAPTAIN! by Walt Whitman

Speaker One:

O Captain! My Captain!

Speaker Two:

By Walt Whitman

Speaker One:

O Captain! my Captain! our fearful trip is done,
The ship has weathr'd every rack,* the prize we sought is won, * suffering

Speaker Three:

The port is near, the bells I hear, the people all exulting,* * showing triumph
While follow eyes the steady keel, the vessel grim and daring;

Class Chorus:

But O heart! heart! heart!
O the bleeding drops of red,
Where on the deck my Captain lies,
Fallen cold and dead.

Speaker Four:

O Captain! my Captain! rise up and hear the bells;
Rise up—for you the flag is flung—for you the bugle trills,

Speaker Five:

For you bouquets and ribbon'd wreaths—for you the shores a-crowding,
For you they call, the swaying mass, their eager faces turning;

Class Chorus:

Here Captain! dear father!
This arm beneath your head!
It is some dream that on the deck,
You've fallen cold and dead.

Speaker Six:

My Captain does not answer, his lips are pale and still,
My father does not feel my arm, he has no pulse nor will,

Speaker Seven:

The ship is anchored safe and sound, its voyage closed and done,
From fearful trip the victor ship comes in with object won;

Class Chorus:

Exult* O shores, and ring O bells! * express triumph
But I, with mournful tread,
Walk the deck my Captain lies,
Fallen cold and dead.

TOPICS FOR CRITICAL THINKING, WRITING, AND ART

1. *O Captain! My Captain!* is an APOSTROPHE—meaning someone is being spoken to who is not present. Who in the poem is being spoken to?

2. The poem uses an extended METAPHOR comparing the president of the United States to the Captain and our country to a ship. In what way might a teacher in a classroom be compared to a captain? If the teacher is the Captain, what might the students be called? What words in the poem refer to a ship?

3. This poem uses very emotional language. Why is emotional language suitable for this poem? Find words or phrases in the poem that are very emotional. Recite a stanza that is very emotional.

4. This has always been a popular poem. Why do so many people appreciate it?

ART: Create the front page of a newspaper with a headline of five words or less telling the world of Lincoln's death.

I WANDERED LONELY AS A CLOUD
by William Wordsworth (1770–1850)

ABOUT THE POEM: A meadow of daffodils brightens the mood of the speaker.

WAYS TO DRAMATIZE

1. INTRODUCING THE POEM: Give students a copy of the poem. Discuss About the Poem. Ask students how a meadow of daffodils and later a memory of it brightens the mood of the speaker. Recite the poem using good articulation and speaking slowly.

2. EVERYBODY DRAMATIZES: Recite each stanza of the poem. Then have students recite the stanza with you. Recite the whole poem with students using gestures.

3. DRAMATIZING IN PAIRS OR GROUPS: Divide the class into groups of four to dramatize the poem. Some students may play inanimate objects. Some may dramatize for the class.

4. PERFORMING: Using costume pieces and instruments, perform the poem for others. Perform it with *In Just-* (another spring poem in this book) or with poems of different seasons. (See Subject Index Across the Curriculum.)

CAST: Narrator, Cloud, Daffodils, Lake, Trees, Stars

COSTUME and PROPS Suggestions: *Daffodils:* Hold paper cut-out daffodils or wear a yellow daffodil hat or collar; *Cloud:* White nylon netting; *Lake:* Filmy blue fabric; *Trees:* Hold or wear green leaves or wear a green-leaf hat.

INSTRUMENT SUGGESTIONS: Use a triangle, wind chimes, and jingle bells to accent the action.

I WANDERED LONELY AS A CLOUD
by William Wordsworth

I wandered lonely as a cloud *(Arms make cloud and sway.)*

That floats on high o'er vales* and hills, *(Raise arms higher. Keep swaying.)* * valleys

When all at once I saw a crowd, *(Open arms in wonder. Shield eyes.)*

A host,* of golden daffodils, *(Arms create daffodils.)* * a multitude or great number

Beside the lake, beneath the trees, *(Arms create lake and then trees.)*

Fluttering and dancing in the breeze. *(Flutter hands and sway.)*

Continuous as the stars that shine *(Arms open out and hands become stars.)*

And twinkle on the milky way, *(Hands twinkle.)*

They stretched in never-ending line *(Make line with arms.)*

Along the margin of a bay; *(Arms make bay.)*

Ten thousand saw I at a glance, *(Flick ten fingers repetitively.)*

Tossing their heads in a sprightly dance. *(Hands dance like daffodils.)*

The waves beside them danced, but they *(Ripple arms joyfully.)*

Outdid the sparkling waves in glee; *(Hands shimmer gleefully.)*

A poet could not be but gay, *(Smile.)*

In such a jocund* company; *(Toss head cheerfully.)* * cheerful

I gazed—and gazed—but little thought *(Look around. Touch head.)*

What wealth the show to me had brought: *(Arms scoop toward body.)*

For oft, when on my couch I lie

In vacant or in pensive* mood, *(Rest head in hands.)*

* dreamily thoughtful

They flash upon that inward eye *(Flash hands by eyes.)*

Which is the bliss of solitude; *(Touch heart. Nod head.)*

And then my heart with pleasure fills, *(Open arms out from heart.)*

And dances with the daffodils. *(Sway like dancing daffodils.)*

TOPICS FOR CRITICAL THINKING, WRITING, AND ART

1. How do you know the speaker in the poem has a good memory and imagination?

2. What is a memory?

3. Wordsworth uses HYPERBOLE (or exaggeration) when he says that he saw "ten thousand daffodils in a glance." Why might he feel he saw this many daffodils and why is the HYPERBOLE effective in this poem?

4. The speaker uses a SIMILE (a comparison using *like* or *as*) when he says he wandered "lonely as a cloud." On what occasions might a person feel "lonely as a cloud"?

5. Wordsworth's poem uses PERSONIFICATION, making the daffodils and the lake act like human beings. For example, both the lake and daffodils dance. And the daffodils are in "a crowd and toss their heads." In what way do daffodils have "heads"? In what way might a lake and daffodils seem to "dance"?

ART: Draw a field of "dancing daffodils." Or create a cartoon of a daffodil personifying it by giving it a head with some human features and making it seem to dance.

CHAPTER ELEVEN
Dramatizing Ballads

The childhood of western civilization is in poetry. It's a self-created folk art.
—Charles Francis Dicken, psychologist, author

ABOUT BALLADS: Folk ballads tell a story in song. They are called "folk" because anonymous folk singers made them up. In the days before most people could read, storytellers traveled to villages and entertained the people by singing stories to them. The singers heard others sing the stories and then made up their own versions, keeping the parts they liked and adding stanzas or scenes. Over time, the most action-packed scenes lasted because the singers remembered the ones that entertained the audience most.

Poets Edgar Allen Poe, Henry Wadsworth Longfellow, and others wrote "art" or "literary ballads," so-called because they were artistically crafted by known authors and followed the ballad form. Usually these "literary ballads" were spoken rather than sung. *The Rime of the Ancient Mariner* by S. T. Coleridge is the most famous literary ballad.

Ballads usually tell the story of one character, and the title is that character's name. Many ballads are serious, dramatic, and include revenge, disappointment in love, supernatural beings and events, death, and characters with great physical strength or agility. Some, though, are amusing, such as the comical *The Ballad of Mr. Fox* in the Performance Script.

THE BALLAD OF JOHN HENRY

Anonymous (Adapted by Louise Thistle)

ABOUT THE BALLAD: John Henry was an African-American steel-driver, the greatest steel-driver the Chesapeake & Ohio Railroad ever had. Scholars believe John Henry really lived, although the events in the ballad story are exaggerated. Around 1870, he was hired to work on the Chesapeake and Ohio's Big Bend Tunnel. Steel driving was back-breaking work. The driver hammered a drill into the rock of a mountain so explosives could be poured in, the rocks' broken up, and a tunnel built.

When a machine was invented to do the job, John Henry's "Captain," the boss tunnel-builder, wanted to try out the machine. So, according to the story, the powerful John Henry and the steam drill were set side by side in a competition to see who could work faster. This contest has been described in songs and stories in different versions for more than 100 years.

WAYS TO DRAMATIZE

1. INTRODUCING THE BALLAD OF JOHN HENRY: Copy the poem for students. Discuss About the Ballad and, if desired, About Ballads, page 161. Recite the ballad slowly focusing on PROJECTION. Have students chant the refrain with you and add other words that seem natural to recite together.

2. EVERYBODY DRAMATIZES: Recite the ballad again with students adding gestures.

3. PAIRS OR GROUPS DRAMATIZE: Choose seven students to read a stanza. Then, divide the class into pairs or groups to dramatize. In pairs, one narrates, while the other plays John Henry. Groups dramatize a stanza or scene. After practicing, pairs or groups could dramatize for the class in sequence.

4. PERFORMING: Have students make or bring in props. Practice again and perform incorporating instruments for others.

CAST: (3 or more): Narrator, John Henry, Mammy, Mountain, Captain, Steam Drill, and Everybody (These roles may be played by one or as many as desired.)

COSTUME AND INSTRUMENT SUGGESTIONS: Railroad-style overalls and an oversize hammer for John Henry; bright floral apron for mother; a railroad cap for the Captain. Use a drum for trudging up the mountain, rattles for "sitting on his mammy's knee," and a wood block for hammering.

THE BALLAD OF JOHN HENRY
adapted by Louise thistle

SCENE ONE
CAST: (3) Narrator, John Henry, Mother

When John Henry was a little baby boy, *(Make self small.)*
Sitting on his mammy's knee; *(Stoop.)*
He picked up a hammer and a little piece of steel, *(Raise hammer in one hand, steel in other.)*
Saying, "Hammer's going to be the death of me, Lord, Lord, *(Raise hammer and chant.)*
Hammer's going to be the death of me."

SCENE 2
CAST: (3) Narrator, Mountain, John Henry

John Henry went up the mountain *(Trudge up hill.)*
And he came down on t'other side. *(Arm sweeps down.)*
The mountain was SOOO tall. *(Show tall peak.)*
John Henry was SOOO small *(Stoop.)*
That he laid down his hammer and he cried, "Lord, Lord." *(Lower hammer, raise hands to Lord and chant.)*
He laid down his hammer and he cried.

SCENE 3
CAST: (2) Narrator, John Henry

John Henry was a man just six feet high, *(Raise hand up.)*
Nearly two feet and a half across the chest. *(Spread arms across chest.)*
He'd take a nine-pound hammer and hammer all day long *(Lift heavy hammer and hammer.)*
And NEVER get tired and want rest, "Lord, Lord" *(Put hand out in gesture of refusal, raise hands on Lord and chant.)*
And NEVER get tired and want rest.

SCENE 4
CAST: (3) Narrator, John Henry, Captain

John Henry said to his Captain, *(Nod.)*
"Captain, please go to Town, *(Point to town.)*
Bring me back a twelve-pound hammer *(Mime raising twelve-pound hammer.)*
And I'll BEAT that steam drill down, Lord, Lord, *(Strike fist into hand on BEAT and chant.)*
I'll BEAT that steam drill down."

SCENE 5
CAST: (4) Narrator, John Henry, Steel Drill (2)

They placed John Henry on the right side, *(Gesture to the right.)*
They put that steam drill on the left; *(Gesture to the left.)*
He said, "Before that steam drill beats ME down *(Point to self on ME.)*
I'll die with my hammer by my chest, Lord, Lord, *(Raise hammer, place across chest and chant.)*
I'll die with my hammer by my chest."

SCENE 6
CAST: (4) Narrator, John Henry, Steel Drill (2)

John Henry hammered on the right side *(Hammer on right side.)*
That steam drill kept driving on the left, *(Vibrate drill on left.)*
John Henry BEAT that steam drill down, *(Lift fist high, sweep it down on BEAT.)*
But, he hammered his poor heart to death, Lord, Lord, *(Touch heart repetitively and chant.)*
He hammered his poor heart to death.

SCENE 7
CAST: (4): Narrator John Henry, Everybody (2)

Well, John Henry was placed by the tunnel *(Gesture toward tunnel.)*
With a marker by his body in the sand. *(Raise marker.)*
Now EVERYBODY riding on a C and O train *(Bow or curtsy.)*
Cries, "There lies our steel-driving man, Lord, Lord. *(Point at earth. Then raise hands and chant.)*
There lies our steel-driving man."

TOPICS FOR CRITICAL THINKING, WRITING, AND ART

1. How does the first stanza show that John Henry was unique?

2. Can a person sometimes work faster than a powerful machine? Explain.

3. The job of steam-driver was taken over by a machine. Do you think it's good that machines often have taken over the hard work once done by people? Explain.

4. A REFRAIN is a verse or a phrase that is repeated. Why do songs and poems have REFRAINS? Why do performers and audiences like REFRAINS?

5. Why are the words "Lord, Lord" repeated at the end of each stanza?

6. John Henry beat the steam drill. Was it worth it? Explain.

7. The *Ballad of John Henry* doesn't have a happy ending, but people have been reading, telling, and singing the story for more than 100 years. Why do you think people want to hear this story?

8. About 100 years ago, the railroad was the major form of travel and perhaps most important means of transportation. Research the background of the song, "I've Been Working on the Railroad." Sing the song and incorporate it into your dramatization.

ART: Study early trains of the time of John Henry. Then, draw a train suitable for the period. Or, draw a powerful John Henry with his hammer.

THE RAVEN *by Edgar Allan Poe (1809–49)*

(Abridged and adapted for dramatization by Louise Thistle)

ABOUT THE BALLAD: At the bewitching hour of midnight, we look into the study of a man whose sweetheart, Lenore, has died. (Poe wrote *The Raven* two years before the death of his young wife, whom he loved intensely and who at the time was very ill.)

WAYS TO DRAMATIZE:

1. INTRODUCING THE BALLAD: Copy the ballad for students. Discuss About the Ballad, and, if desired, About Ballads, page 161. Recite the poem using good articulation. The class recites the Raven's lines with you.

2. EVERYBODY DRAMATIZES: Recite the whole ballad with students adding gestures and "tapping."

3. PAIRS OR GROUPS DRAMATIZE: Discuss ways to dramatize the poem in groups. The Man (the "ponderer" throughout the poem) might memorize the poem with the Raven saying its lines. Then, divide the class into groups of four to dramatize one or more stanzas or the whole poem. After practicing, dramatize the stanzas in sequence or choose groups to perform the whole poem.

4. PERFORMING: Have students make or bring in costumes and props. Use instruments to perform the poem again.

CAST: Narrator: A dignified gentleman; Raven with a stately bearing

COSTUME, PROPS AND INSTRUMENT SUGGESTIONS: *Man:* Dignified gentleman's dark outfit; *Raven:* Black cloth or cape (or use a shadow puppet); *Bust of Pallas:* Use a portrait; *Streaming Lamplight:* Gold tinsel on a stick.

INSTUMENT SUGGESTIONS: Use wood block, rattles, a triangle, or vocal sound effects.

THE RAVEN by Edgar Allan Poe
Abridged and adapted for dramatization by Louise Thistle

SCENE 1

Narrator:
THE RAVEN
By Edgar Allan Poe

Once upon a midnight dreary, while I pondered, weak and weary, *(Shake head.)*
Over many a quaint and curious volume of forgotten lore— *(Show open book.)*
While I nodded, nearly napping, suddenly there came a tapping, *(Nod. Then, tap.)*
As of some one gently rapping, rapping at my chamber door. *(Rap.)*
Man:
" 'Tis some visitor," I muttered, "tapping at my chamber door— *(Tap.)*
Only this, and nothing more." *(Shake head.)*

SCENE 2

Narrator:
Ah, distinctly I remember, it was in the bleak December; *(Hold up index finger.)*
And each separate dying ember wrought its ghost upon the floor. *(Shimmer fingers on "dying ember.")*
Eagerly I wished the morrow—vainly I had sought to borrow
From my books surcease* of sorrow—sorrow for the lost Lenore— *(Show open book.)*
For the rare and radiant maiden whom the angels name Lenore— *(Point up on "angels.")*
Nameless *here* forevermore.

SCENE 3

Narrator:

Deep into that darkness peering, long I stood there, wondering, fearing,
(Lean forward, peer.)
Doubting, dreaming dreams no mortals ever dared to dream before;
(Shake head.)
But the silence was unbroken, and the stillness gave no token, *(Touch lips.)*
And the only word there spoken was the whispered word,

Man: *(Stage whisper.)*

Lenore"?

Narrator:

This I whispered, and an echo murmured back the word,

Raven: *(Out of view.)*

"Lenore!"

Narrator:

Merely this, and nothing more.

SCENE 4

Narrator:

Back into the chamber turning, all my soul within me burning, *(Turn head. Fist touches heart.)*
Soon again I heard a tapping something louder than before. *(Tap louder.)*

Man:

"Surely," said I, "surely, that is something at my window lattice; *(Hands make window.)*
Let me see, then, what thereat is, and this mystery explore—
Let my heart be still a moment, and this mystery explore— *(Touch heart.)*
'Tis the wind and nothing more!" *(Hands create wind.)*

SCENE 5

Narrator:

Open here I flung the shutter, when, with many a flirt and flutter, *(Open shutter.)*

In there stepped a stately Raven of the saintly days of yore; *(Step forward assuredly.)*

Not the least obeisance made he; not a minute stopped or stayed he;

But with a mien* of lord or lady, perched above my chamber door— *(Point above door.)*

Perched upon a bust of Pallas,* just above my chamber door—

Perched, and sat, and nothing more. *(Cock head and stare.)*

SCENE 6

Narrator:

Then this ebony bird beguiling my sad fancy into smiling *(Smile.)*

By the grave and stern decorum of the countenance it wore, *(Stare piercingly.)*

Man:

"Though thy crest be shorn and shaven, thou," I said, "art sure no craven,

Ghastly grim and ancient Raven wandering from the Nightly shore—

Tell me what thy lordly name is on the Night's Plutonian* shore!" *(Hands show expanse of night and then point to Hell.)*

Raven: *(Shaking head.)*

Quoth the raven, "Nevermore."

SCENE 7

Narrator:

But the raven, sitting lonely on that placid bust, spoke only

That one word, as if his soul in that one word he did outpour. *(Point to heart and then raise index finger.)*

Nothing farther then he uttered—not a feather then he fluttered—

Till I scarcely more than muttered,

Man:

"Other friends have flown before—

On the morrow *he* will leave me, as my Hopes have flown before."

Raven: *(Shaking head.)*

Then the bird said, "Nevermore."

SCENE 8

Narrator:

And the raven, never flitting, still is sitting, *still* is sitting
On the pallid bust of Pallas just above my chamber door; *(Point to bust.)*
And his eyes have all the seeming of a demon's that is dreaming, *(Eyes menace.)*
And the lamp–light o'er him streaming throws the shadow on the floor; *(Hands create streaming light.)*
And my soul from out that shadow that lies floating on the floor
Shall be lifted—nevermore! *(Raise hands up. Then shake head.)*

***surcease:** leave off from, cease
***mien:** bearing, demeanor, look of
***Pallas:** Greek Goddess of wisdom
***Plutonian:** Pluto was Roman god of Hades and ruled the world of the dead.

TOPICS FOR CRITICAL THINKING, WRITING, AND ART

1.Who are the characters in the poem? Some believe Lenore is a character even though she never appears. What do you think? Explain.

2. Edgar Allan Poe believes that poetry should be based on the truth of the emotions and music. What kinds of emotions does Poe create in *The Raven?*

3. In lines one and three of every stanza, *The Raven* uses INTERNAL RHYME (or words within a line that rhyme). For example in the first stanza, line one has *dreary/ weary* and line three, *napping/tapping.* Find the INTERNAL RHYME in lines one and three in the other stanzas. Mark the rhyming words in the lines and say them aloud.

4. Poe uses the musical device of ALLITERATION or words close together beginning with the same consonant sound. For example, line three in stanza one has *nodded, nearly,* and *napping.* All the other stanzas of *The Raven* have ALLITERATION. Find the lines with alliteration in each stanza. Read them aloud to experience their musicality. Which line of the poem has five alliterative words?

5. What is the effect of ending each stanza with either "nothing more," "forevermore" and finally, "nevermore"?

6. Poe felt that the word *nevermore* had a powerfully melancholy sound and used the word for a sound of gloom and despair. What other words in the poem have the sound quality of despair?

7. What does the raven represent? Is he a symbol of good or evil or something else? Explain.

8. What words in the poem are often quoted? Why do you think people like saying them or find them hard to forget?

ART: Imagine you are staging *The Raven* as a play or film. Describe the lighting, set, and costumes you'd use. Draw a picture illustrating your ideas.

ANNABEL LEE *by Edgar Allan Poe (1809–49)*

Adapted for dramatization by Louise Thistle

ABOUT THE BALLAD: The speaker recalls his love of a beautiful young woman who died at the height of their love.

WAYS TO DRAMATIZE

1. INTRODUCING THE BALLAD: Copy the ballad for students. Discuss About the Ballad and, if desired, About Ballads, page 161. Recite the ballad slowly using good articulation.

2. EVERYBODY DRAMATIZES: Recite the poem with students. Recite the poem again with students adding gestures. Choose six students to each recite a stanza. Have the class play the Chorus.

3. PAIRS OR GROUPS DRAMATIZE: Using the cast list for each stanza, divide the students into pairs or groups to dramatize stanzas or the whole ballad. Some groups may dramatize for the class.

4. PERFORMING: Using costume pieces and music have highly motivated students perform in groups or pairs for others. (In pairs, one might play the Narrator and the other Annabel Lee, doing graceful, slow-motion movements throughout to depict her spirit.)

CAST: Narrator, Annabel Lee, Sea, Seraphs, Wind, Cloud, Highborn Kinsmen, Sepulchre, Moon

COSTUME SUGGESTIONS: *Annabel Lee:* Flowing long white skirt and blouse *Narrator:* All black clothing; *Sea:* Strips of filmy blue material or long scarves waved; *Seraphs (who are also called Angels and Highborn Kinsmen):* Black capes; *Moon:* Moon headpiece with cardboard crescent moon covered in tinfoil or hold up a cutout of the moon; *Cloud:* Small piece of white nylon netting

MUSIC SUGGESTIONS: Claude Debussy's *La Mar* or *Clair de Lune* played while the poem is recited.

ANNABEL LEE by Edgar Allan Poe
Adapted for dramatization by Louise Thistle

SCENE 1
CAST: (4) Narrator, Two Seas, Annabel Lee

It was many and many a year ago,
Chorus: **In a kingdom by the sea,** *(Arms make castle and then make waves.)*
That a maiden there lived whom you may know
By the name of Annabel Lee; *(Curtsy.)*
And this maiden she lived with no other thought *(Point to head.)*
Than to love and be loved by me. *(Touch heart to rhythm of the words three times.)*

SCENE 2
CAST: (4) Narrator, Annabel Lee, Two Seraphs

***She* was a child and *I* was a child,** *(Gesture out and then to self.)*
Chorus: **In this kingdom by the sea,** *(Arms make castle and then make waves.)*
But we loved with a love that was more than love— *(Fists by heart three times.)*
I and my Annabel Lee— *(Gesture to self.)*
With a love that the wingéd seraphs* of Heaven *(Make wings.)* *highest rank of angels
Coveted her and me. *(Hands reach out and grab.)*

SCENE 3
CAST: (4) Narrator, Sea, Wind, Cloud, Annabel Lee, Highborn Kinsmen, (double small roles)

And this was the reason that, long ago, *(Raise index finger.)*
Chorus: **In this kingdom by the sea,** *(Arms make castle and then make waves.)*
A wind blew out of a cloud by night *(Arms create wind.)*
Chilling my beautiful Annabel Lee; *(Shiver.)*
So that her highborn kinsmen came *(Pull arms toward body.)*

And bore her away from me, *(Arms up, palms up.)*
To shut her up in a sepulchre* *(Hands press forward.)* *Tomb
Chorus: **In this kingdom by the sea.** *(Arms make castle and then, waves.)*

SCENE 4
CAST: (4) Narrator, Two Angels, Annabel Lee

The angels, not half so happy in Heaven, *(Arms make wings. Freeze.)*
Went envying her and me: *(Squint in envy.)*
Yes! that was the reason (as all men know, *(Raise index finger.)*
Chorus: **In this kingdom by the sea)** *(Arms make castle and then waves.)*
That the wind came out of the cloud, *(Arms create wind.)*
Chilling and killing my Annabel Lee. *(Shiver. Drop head.)*

SCENE 5
CAST: (4) Narrator, Two Demons, Annabel Lee

But our love it was stronger by far than the love *(Make strong arms.)*
Of those who were older than we— *(Slump.)*
Of many far wiser than we—*(Point to head.)*
Nor the demons down under the sea, *(Stoop. Make cruel hands.)*
Can ever dissever my soul from the soul *(Hands tear, then touch heart twice.)*
Of the beautiful Annabel Lee:

SCENE 6
CAST: (4) Narrator, Moon, Annabel Lee, Two Seas (Moon also plays one Sea.)

For the moon never beams without bringing me dreams *(Arms make moon, rest head in hands.)*
Of the beautiful Annabel Lee;
And the stars never rise but I see the bright eyes *(Hands make rising stars. Touch eyes.)*
Of the beautiful Annabel Lee;
And so, all the night-tide, I lie down by the side *(Arms make waves. Hands rest on head.)*
Of my darling, my darling, my life and my bride, *(Point to heart three times.)*
In the sepulchre* there by the sea— *(Hands together in prayer.)*
In her tomb by the sounding sea. *(Hands together in prayer. Then, arms make waves. Freeze.)*

TOPICS FOR CRITICAL THINKING, WRITING, AND ART

1. *Annabel Lee* is one of the favorite poems of the English language. Why do you think people like it so much?

2. Some lines of the poem are so musical that people memorize them without trying. Which lines do you find most musical? Which lines do you like saying best?

3. Poe uses the words to create a rhythm that imitates the sound of waves rolling in on the seashore. Which lines are the most rhythmical?

4. The speaker is obsessed with his memory of Annabel Lee. Do you think his feeling and mourning are excessive? Why do you think he feels so strongly about her? Why can't he forget her?

5. The predominant words throughout the poem are *sea, Lee, me* and *we.* Why do you think Poe poet emphasizes these words?

6. Read *The Raven* another poem by Poe in this book about a man haunted by the death of a young woman he loved. How is the mood and ending different in the poems? Are the poems similar in mood in any way?

ART: Draw a picture to illustrate the poem or an IMAGE from the poem.

RICHARD CORY
by Edward Arlington Robinson (1869–1935)

ABOUT THE BALLAD: Everybody admires the handsome wealthy Richard Cory and wishes they were he, but they learn looks may be deceiving.

WAYS TO DRAMATIZE

1. INTRODUCING THE BALLAD: Copy the ballad for students. Discuss About the Ballad and, if desired, About Ballads, page 161. Recite the poem and discuss it with students.

2. EVERYBODY DRAMATIZES: Recite the poem with students.

3. PAIRS OR GROUPS DRAMATIZE: Individual students (representing the townspeople) each recite a Narrator line. One student is Richard Cory. (If you have more than seventeen students, double up some lines.) Then, dramatize the poem in groups, dividing up the narrator lines among group members. Some groups might dramatize for the class.

4. PERFORMING: Perform using period nineteenth-century costume pieces or contemporary clothing. Richard Cory might sit facing the audience looking self-possessed until the end when he stands and turns his back to the audience and drops his head down symbolizing death.

CAST: Richard Cory, Townspeople/Narrators (scripted for seventeen, but as many as desired)

COSTUME SUGGESTIONS: *Richard Cory:* Period top hat, black suit, and white ruffled shirt or use an elegant suit or jacket for a modern Richard Cory; *Townspeople:* Working-class hats or clothing.

RICHARD CORY by Edward Arlington Robinson

Narrator 1:

Richard Cory

By Edward Arlington Robinson

Narrator 2:

Whenever Richard Cory went down town, *(Gesture to downtown.)*

Narrator 3:

We people on the pavement looked at him: *(Nod.)*

Narrator 4:

He was a gentleman from sole to crown, *(Point to foot and then head.)*

Narrator 5:

Clean favored, and imperially slim. *(Hands show width of waist.)*

Narrator 6:

And he was always quietly arrayed, *(Touch jacket shoulders.)*

Narrator 7:

And he was always human when he talked;

Narrator 8:

But still he fluttered pulses when he said, *(Wiggle hands.)*

Richard Cory:

"Good-morning,"

Narrator 9:

and he glittered when he walked. *(Stride assuredly.)*

Narrator 10:

And he was rich—yes richer than a king— *(Hands make crown.)*

Narrator 11:

And admirably schooled in every grace: *(Bow.)*

Narrator 12:

In fine, we thought that he was everything *(Open out hands.)*

Narrator 13:

To make us wish that we were in his place. *(Point to self and then to Cory.)*

Narrator 14:

So on we worked, and waited for the light, *(Point up to light.)*

Narrator 15:

And went without the meat, and cursed the bread; *(Hands make fists.)*

Narrator 16:

And Richard Cory, one calm summer night,

Narrator 17:

Went home and put a bullet through his head. *(Touch head quickly.)*

TOPICS FOR CRITICAL THINKING, WRITING, AND ART

1. This poem was written in 1896. The topic is upsetting. Why is the poem still printed? Why do many people respond to it?

2. Give four favorable descriptions of Richard Cory in the poem.

3. What is the most dramatic line in the poem? What makes it dramatic in relation to what's happened before?

4. Why might have Richard Cory killed himself?

5. Why is Richard Cory's death particularly unexpected and shocking?

6. What might the people in the town learn from Richard Cory's death?

7. What is the RHYME SCHEME in this poem? Mark and say the rhyming words in each stanza.

ART: Draw a picture of Richard Cory and write on your drawing one or more lines from the poem that describe him.

CHAPTER TWELVE

Dramatizing Nonsense Verse

Poets test words for sounds. So, poetry reaches its ultimate objective only when read aloud.
—Charlotte Lee, author of *Oral Interpretation*

ABOUT NONSENSE VERSE: Nonsense verse is a variety of light verse enjoyable because of its bouncy rhythm, enjoyable sounds, and lack of logic. It's called "light" because it treats all situations, even the most unsettling in a light-hearted frolicsome way. Mother Goose rhymes (dramatized in Chapter 6, Model Lesson page 43) and Limericks (see Chapter Nine, pages 67–75) are forms of nonsense verse.

Nonsense writers frequently use coined (made-up) words, such as an "*uffish* thought," "*tulgey woods*" and "*vorpal* sword" in Lewis Carroll's *Jabberwocky.* Nonsense poems also use words from other languages, tongue twisters, and unusual arrangements of print on the page—anything fun that contributes to the nonsense.

Some of the best nonsense verse is by Lewis Carroll, an English writer and a Mathematical Lecturer at Christ Church College Oxford. As a child, Carroll published a magazine to amuse his family. The first edition, *Useful and Instructive Poetry,* had limericks and a humorous ballad called *Never Stew Your Sister.* Carroll illustrated his magazine with drawings that were unsophisticated but often very funny.

Lewis Carroll is most known for his imaginative books, *Alice's Adventures in Wonderland* and *Through the Looking Glass*. Lewis Carroll wrote these books to entertain Alice Liddell, the daughter of the master of his college, on afternoon rowing excursions on the river Thames. The two selections dramatized here are from these books.

JABBERWOCKY *by Lewis Carroll (1832–98)*

ABOUT THE POEM: In Lewis Carroll's book, *Through the Looking Glass*, Alice steps through a mirror into a "reverse world." Alice finds this poem in a "mirror-book," which was written backwards. The poem tells of a boy going off on a dangerous adventure and uses a lot of strange-sounding words.

WAYS TO DRAMATIZE

1. INTRODUCING THE POEM: Copy the poem for students. Discuss About the Poem and, if desired, About Nonsense Verse, page 180.

2. EVERYBODY DRAMATIZES: Recite each line focusing on good articulation and creating an exuberant and dramatic mood; have the students repeat each line with you. Have students read aloud the explanation of the nonsense words in the About the Nonsense Words section, page 184. Recite the whole poem again with students adding gestures.

3. PAIRS OR GROUPS DRAMATIZE: Ask students to suggest how to dramatize the poem as a play. Have students share movements that express some of the nonsense words. Then, divide students into groups of four to dramatize the whole poem or stanzas. (Some groups may decide to dramatize many of the characters and others only the central ones.) If there are more than four characters in a stanza, double some roles. Have some groups dramatize for the class.

4. PERFORMING: Using props and costumes, perform the poem for others. Perhaps include *Father William,* another Carroll poem in this book and other nonsense poems by Carroll.

CAST: Narrator, Toves, Borogoves, mome raths, Son, the son's Teacher or grandfather, the Jabberwocky

COSTUME AND PROP SUGGESTIONS: *Son:* Baseball cap or perhaps crown symbolizing his heroic role, yardstick or dowel as "vorpal" sword; *Jabberwocky:* Black or brown fabric, (perhaps shaggy or wooly); *Grandfather:* Yardstick or other cane, perhaps a beard and cloak. *Other Nonsense Characters*: Bright-colored cloths, feather boas, or atmosphere sticks. Use your imagination.

JABBERWOCKY by Lewis Carroll

SCENE 1
CAST: Narrator, Slithy Toves, Wabe, Borogroves, Mome Raths

Jabberwocky
By Lewis Carroll
(Create your own imaginative gestures for this stanza.)
'Twas brillig, and the slithy toves
Did gyre and gimble in the wabe;
All mimsy were the borogoves,
And the mome raths outgrabe.

SCENE 2
CAST: Narrator, Grandfather, Son (the Hero), Jubjub bird, Bandersnatch

"Beware the Jabberwocky, my son! *(Wag finger.)*
The jaws that bite, the claws that catch! *(Look menacing, bite. Hands make claws.)*
Beware the Jubjub bird, and shun *(Make strange wings.)*
The frumious Bandersnatch!" *(Shield face with arms.)*

SCENE 3
CAST: Narrator, Hero, Tumtum tree

He took his vorpal sword in hand: *(Grab sword.)*
Long time the manxome foe he sought— *(Look all around.)*
So rested he by the Tumtum tree, *(Rest head. Arms create tree.)*
And stood awhile in thought. *(Point rhythmically to head.)*

SCENE 4
CAST: Narrator, Hero, Jabberwocky

And as in uffish thought he stood, *(Point to head with other finger.)*
The Jabberwocky, with eyes of flame, *(Thrust head forward. Eyes blaze.)*
Came whiffling through the tulgey wood, *(Bounce sideways.)*
And burbled as it came! *(Burble.)*

SCENE 5
CAST: Narrator, Hero, Jabberwocky

One, two! One, two! And through and through *(Jab with sword.)*
The vorpal blade went snicker-snack! *(Wave arms in cutting motion.)*
He left it dead, and with its head *(Point to dead Jabberwocky. Raise its head up.)*
He went galumphing back. *(Bounce awkwardly.)*

SCENE 6
CAST: Narrator, Hero, Grandfather

"And hast thou slain the Jabberwock? *(Reach index finger high.)*
Come to my arms, my beamish boy! *(Open arms.)*
O frabjous day! Callooh! Callay!" *(Toss arms up.)*
He chortled in his joy. *(Chortle.)*

SCENE 7
CAST: Narrator, Slithy Toves, Wabe, Borogroves, Mome Raths

'Twas brillig and the slithy toves *(Repeat gestures from first stanza.)*
Did gyre and gimble in the wabe;
All mimsy were the borogoves,
And the mome raths outgrabe."

ABOUT THE NONSENSE WORDS IN JABBERWOCKY

Someone wrote to Lewis Carroll and asked what *Jabberwocky* meant. Carroll replied: "I'm very much afraid that I didn't mean anything but nonsense! Still, you know, words mean more than we mean to express when we use them; so a good book ought to mean a great deal more than the writer meant."

Humpty Dumpty tells Alice in the book *Through the Looking Glass* that *Jabberwocky* has "portmanteau words." (A *portmanteau* is a suitcase with two parts. A "portmanteau word" then has two meanings packed into one word—for example, *brunch* is a combination of *breakfast* and *lunch. Smog* combines the words *smoke* and *fog.*) Here are some of the explanations Humpty gives Alice on the meaning of some of the "portmanteau words" in *Jabberwocky.*

Brillig means four o'clock in the afternoon—the time when you begin broiling things for dinner.

Slithy means "lithe and slimy."

Lithe is the same as active.

Toves are something like badgers and something like lizards and they're something like corkscrews. Also they make their nests under sundials and live on cheese.

Gyre is to go round and round like a gyroscope.

Gimble means to gimble and to make holes like a gimlet.

The Wabe is the grass plot round a sundial. It's called a wabe because it goes a long way before it, and a long way behind it.

Mimsy is flimsy and miserable.

A Borogove is a thin, shabby-looking bird with its feathers sticking out all round—something like a live mop.

A mome rath: *mome* is short for "from home" and *rath* is a sort of green pig.

Outgribing is between bellowing and whistling with a kind of sneeze in the middle.

Uffish thought: state of mind when the voice is gruffish, the manner roughish, and the temper huffish.

Burble: to burble you take three verbs—*bleat, murmur* and *warble.*

Fumious: Take fuming and furious and get furious-fuming, but if you have the rarest of gifts, a perfectly balanced mind, you will say "fumious."

TOPICS FOR CRITICAL THINKING, WRITING, AND ART

1. Read the explanation of "portmanteau words" in the About the Nonsense Words, page 180. Then, find five of your favorite "portmanteau words."

2. Make up your own "portmanteau words," such as *grare* that's a combination of *growl* and *glare* or *crounce* that combines *crush* and *bounce.*

3. This poem is "mock heroic" meaning that it makes fun of what might be a serious dangerous adventure. Describe what's humorous about the Jabberwocky, the enemy in the poem.

4. People say that the poem *Jabberwocky* is not completely nonsense because in parts the story makes sense. What parts of the poem make sense? Which parts seem most nonsensical?

5. Why do you think the first stanza is repeated at the end?

ART: Study the illustration of the Jabberwocky by John Tenniell in Lewis Carroll's book, *Through the Looking Glass.* Draw your own interpretation of the monster.

FATHER WILLIAM
by Lewis Carroll (1832–1898)

ABOUT THE POEM: As a child, Lewis Carrol liked to write poem "parodies" that imitated and mocked serious poems. *Father William* is a parody of a poem by Robert Southey in which a stern old man gives very serious advice to his teenage son on how to live a long healthful life. *Father William* is in Lewis Carroll's *Alice's Adventures in Wonderland.*

WAYS TO DRAMATIZE

1. INTRODUCING THE POEM: Copy the poem for students. Discuss About the Poem and, if desired, About Nonsense Verse, page 180. Recite the poem focusing on good articulation and changing your vocal tone to portray the two characters.

2. EVERYBODY DRAMATIZES: Recite the whole poem again with students.

3. PAIRS OR GROUPS DRAMATIZE: Divide the class into two groups. Group One plays the young man and Group Two, Father William. Reverse the roles. Next, divide the class into pairs to dramatize the poem. Some groups could dramatize for the class

4. PERFORMING: Use props and costumes and perform the poem for others. Memorize the dialogue. Perhaps also perform *Jabberwocky* (another Carroll poem in this book) and other nonsense poems by Carroll.

CAST(2): Young Man, Father William

COSTUME AND PROP SUGGESTIONS: *Young Man*: Baseball cap; *Father William:* black derby, bowler, or gentleman's hat.

FATHER WILLIAM by Lewis Carroll

Picture adapted from John Tenniell.

Young Man:

"You are old, Father William," the young man said, *(Hands on hips.)*
"And your hair has become very white; *(Point to his hair.)*
And yet you incessantly stand on your head— *(Point to his head.)*
Do you think, at your age, it is right?" *(Open arms out in question.)*

Father William:

"In my youth," Father William replied to his son, *(Nod head.)*
"I feared it might injure the brain; *(Point to brain.)*
But now that I'm perfectly sure I have none, *(Shake head. Point to brain.)*
Why, I do it again and again." *(Say "again" with long* a *as British do.)*

Young Man:

"You are old," said the youth, "as I mentioned before, *(Hands on hips.)*
And have grown most uncommonly fat; *(Make belly with arms.)*
Yet you turned a back-somersault in at the door— *(Make somersault motion with hands.)*
Pray, what is the reason for that?" *(Open arms out in question.)*

Father William:

"In my youth," said the sage, as he shook his gray locks, *(Shake locks.)*
"I kept all my limbs very supple *(Pat limbs.)*
By the use of this ointment—one shilling the box— *(Hold up index finger.)*
Allow me to sell you a couple?" *(Take a couple of boxes out of your pocket.)*

Young Man:

"You are old," said the youth, "and your jaws are too weak *(Chew.)*
For anything tougher than suet;* *(Chew slowly.)*
Yet you finished the goose, with the bones and the beak— *(Make wings, touch bones and hands make beak.)*
Pray, how did you manage to do it?" *(Open arms out in wonder.)*

* hard fat around loins of pork or beef

Father William:

"In my youth," said his father, "I took to the law, *(Open law book.)*
And argued each case with my wife; *(Point indignantly.)*
And the muscular strength, which it gave to my jaw, *(Rub jaw.)*
Has lasted the rest of my life." *(Open arms out in certainty.)*

Young Man:

"You are old," said the youth; "one would hardly suppose
That your eye was as steady as ever; *(Point to his eye.)*
Yet you balanced an eel on the end of your nose— *(Make twisting eel on nose.)*
What made you so awfully clever?" *(Open arms out in wonder.)*

Father William:

"I have answered three questions, and that is enough," *(Hold up three fingers.)*
Said his father, "Don't give yourself airs! *(Stick nose in air.)*
Do you think I can listen all day to such stuff? *(Wag finger.)*
Be off, or I'll kick you downstairs!" *(Pretend to kick.)*

TOPICS FOR CRITICAL THINKING, WRITING, AND ART

1. Nonsense verse often rhymes. Find the rhyming words in each stanza. What is the RHYME SCHEME?

2. This poem has two characters. Who are the two characters? What are their characteristics?

3. This poem is considered nonsense. Find the most nonsensical incident of the poem and recite it.

ART: Study the illustrations of *Father William* by John Tenniell in *Alice's Adventures in Wonderland.* Then, make a cartoon drawing of one of the incidents in the poem.

CHAPTER THIRTEEN

Dramatizing Historical Narrative Poetry

Allow your body, voice and emotions a wide range of expression,
and stretch yourself into the heightened world of poetic imagination.
—Jonathan McMurtry, actor

ABOUT HISTORICAL NARRATIVE POETRY: Story or Narrative Poetry tells a story in verse. Originally most stories rhymed. In the days before people could read, storytellers traveled to villages and told stories. The rhyme helped the storytellers remember the action and made the stories memorable and enjoyable to the listeners.

Story poems were a way to pass down history and values and to inform people of what was happening in society. For example, the Greek poet, Homer, told of heroic deeds of warriors in the Trojan war in *The Iliad.* In *Paul Revere's Ride,* Henry Wadsworth Longfellow tells his version of Paul Revere's ride to warn Americans that the British were coming to seize Americans' weapons.

PAUL REVERE'S RIDE
by Henry Wadsworth Longfellow (1807–82)

ABOUT THE POEM: *Paul Revere's Ride* tells the story of Paul Revere's famous ride on April 18, 1775. Then, America was made up of thirteen colonies. The colonies were ruled by Britain. Most Americans were from Britain, but some felt they shouldn't be under British rule. They disliked the taxes and the laws imposed by Britain. They wanted to rule themselves.

Paul Revere was one of those who spoke out against the English king and government. He and others felt that a war inevitably would come between Britain and America. These Americans stored arms to prepare for a war, but the British planned to seize them. Revere didn't know, however, which route the British would take from Boston to seize the weapons—by boat across the Charles River or by land.

Revere's friend, Robert Newman, was assigned to watch from the tower of the Old North Church. He saw the British go in boats across the Charles River and signaled Revere and others.

Revere was one of a number of riders in a kind of relay assigned to "spread the alarm" that the British were coming. Thus began the first battle in the American Revolution, which ultimately resulted in freeing Americans from British rule.

Henry Wadsworth Longfellow was one of the last great storytelling poets. He published *Paul Revere's Ride* in 1861 in *Tales of a Wayside Inn,* a book of story poems. In the book, travelers sit in an inn and tell each other stories. *Paul Revere's Ride* is *The Landlord's Tale.*

This literary ballad tells of the midnight ride of Paul Revere from Charlestown to Lexington and Concord to warn the people of the approach of British troops at the outbreak of the Revolution. The poem, which created an American legend, is in some respects inaccurate. Revere never actually waited for signals from lanterns, and it was "a young Dr. Prescott" who carried the news to Concord, while Revere went to Lexington. Revere, however, masterminded the plan so he deserves the credit as hero. Revere was not particularly well known during his life time and became a national hero only after the publication of this poem.

The poem is a metrical tale meaning that it is a story in rhythmic meter and rhyme. Its rhythm is like the galloping of hoofbeats. The poem is exciting to dramatize because of its dramatic action, bold exciting hero, and suspenseful atmosphere.

WAYS TO DRAMATIZE

1. Introducing the Poem: Copy the poem for students. Discuss About the Poem and, if desired, About Historical Narrative Poetry. Recite the poem using good projection and articulation. Discuss unknown words and difficult passages.
2. Everybody Dramatizes: Recite sections from the beginning of the poem and then have students recite the sections with you practicing good articulation and projection.
3. Pairs or Groups Dramatize: The poem is scripted and divided into five scenes. (Roles and suggested rhythm instruments for each scene are in the script.) Divide students into five groups. Each group dramatizes one of the five scenes. The teacher assigns the roles using the numbered list. Groups practice and then perform their dramatizations in sequence.
4. Performing: Use costumes and instruments to perform the poem for others. As part of a patriotic program use other patriotic poetry and songs such as "America the Beautiful" (dramatized on pages 237–239 in the Performance Script).

CAST:

STORYTELLER 1 (leader, very responsible, strong voice)
STORYTELLERS 2, 3, 4 (strong voices, ability to follow and pick up cues)
APRIL 18, 1875 SIGN HOLDER
PAUL REVERE (leading role, committed, energetic, strong voice)
HIS FRIEND (leading role, committed, agile)
NORTH CHURCH SIGN HOLDER
CHARLESTOWN SIGN HOLDER
CHARLES RIVER (2)
MOON / MOONLIGHT
SOMERSET, BRITISH MAN-OF-WAR SHIP
MARCHING GRENADIERS (Six or more)
CAPTAIN OF GRENADIERS
PIGEONS (2)
ROOFS (4 or more)
PAUL'S HORSE (stylized movements, Revere's soul mate, dedicated to the cause)
SPARK (kindling into flame)
MEDFORD SIGN HOLDER
COCK
DOG
FOG (2)

LEXINGTON SIGN HOLDER
GILDED WEATHERCOCK
MEETING-HOUSE WINDOWS
FLOCK OF SHEEP (4 or more)
CONCORD SIGN HOLDER
TWITTERING BIRDS

SOUND CREW:
Sound Crew 1: Triangle
Sound Crew 2: Wood block
Sound Crew 3: Maraca and drum
Sound Crew 4: Maraca and gong (or pot lid and metal spoon)
Sound Crew 5: Tambourine
Sound Crew 6: Guiro, jingle bells, taped music (optional)

NOTE: A piano might replace the triangle or make some of the other effects.

OPTIONAL: "Yankee Doodle" or other appropriate American patriotic instrumental music played on a tape recorder or CD operated by the Sound Crew.

BASIC STAGE SETUP:
The actors sit in chairs arranged in a semicircle in view of the audience. Costumes and props are stored under the actors' chairs so they can be taken off and put on when needed.

Downstage is Boston. Upstage is Charlestown. Center stage is the Charles River. The North Church is up right. It might be a table (with a chair on one side to climb the tower) or a ladder that is labeled, North Church.

The Sound Crew sits with instruments on a table to the right of the stage area, in view of the audience. The tables are set so that the Crew can see the stage. See diagram below.

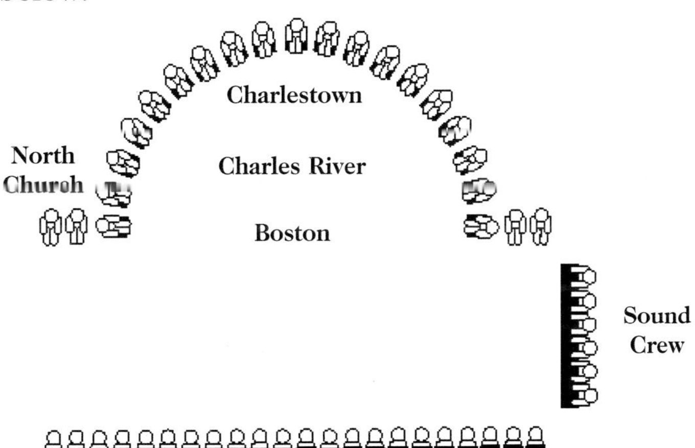

PAUL REVERE'S RIDE by Henry Wadsworth Longfellow
(Adapted and abridged for dramatization by Louise Thistle)

SCENE ONE
Characters: Four storytellers, Revere, Friend, Charlestown Sign Holder, Moon, Somerset Ship

NOTE: The performance might begin with an instrumental version of "Yankee Doodle" or other appropriate American patriotic music.

(Sound Crew 1 strikes triangle three times to begin the drama.)

STORYTELLER 1:
Paul Revere's Ride

(Sound Crew 1 strikes triangle.)

STORYTELLER 1:
By Henry Wadsworth Longfellow

(Sound Crew 1 strikes triangle.)

STORYTELLER 1 (*Cupping ear and gesturing to audience.)*
Listen, my children, and you shall hear

CHORUS: *(Cupping ear and gesturing to audience.)*
LISTEN, my children, and you shall hear

STORYTELLER 1: *(Holding imaginary reins and galloping rhythmically or slapping knees.)*
Of the midnight ride of Paul Revere,

CHORUS: *(Holding imaginary reins and galloping.)*
Of the midnight ride of Paul Revere,

(SOUND CREW 2 strikes wood block simulating hoofbeats. Chorus slap knees.)

STORYTELLER 2:
On the eighteenth of April, in Seventy-five;

(SOUND CREW 1 strikes triangle twice as SIGN HOLDER holds up April 18, 1775 sign.)

STORYTELLER 2:
Hardly a man is now alive
Who remembers that famous day and year.

STORYTELLER 3:
He said to his friend,

(REVERE and FRIEND step center.)

REVERE: *(Forcefully.)*
"If the British march
By land or sea from the town tonight,
(Pointing at tower.) **Hang a lantern aloft in the belfry arch**[1]
Of the North Church tower as a signal light
(Holding up one finger, then two.) **One, if by land, and two, if by sea;**

(SOUND CREW 1 strikes triangle once on "one" and twice on "two.")

REVERE: *(Pointing to self and Charlestown.)*
And I on the Charlestown[2] **shore will be,**

(SOUND CREW 1 strikes triangle as CHARLESTOWN SIGN holds sign in Charlestown area.)

REVERE: *(Imitating riding.)*
Ready to ride and spread the alarm
Through every Middlesex[3] **village and farm,** *(Gesturing broadly length of stage.)*
(Thrusting arm high.) **For the country folk to be up and to arm."**

STORYTELLER 4:
Then he waved Goodnight!
And with muffled[4] **oar**
Silently rowed to the Charlestown shore,

(REVERE and FRIEND wave. Revere mimes rowing using an office chair with wheels. Facing the audience, and moving the chair upstage with feet to Charlestown, with arms simulating rowing. CHARLES RIVER ripples fabric on each side of the boat as SOUND CREW 5 shakes tambourine for rowing.)

STORYTELLER 1:

Just as the MOON rose over the bay,

(SOUND CREW 1 strikes triangle three times for rising. MOON slowly rises up center and freezes—remaining until SOMERSET sits.)

STORYTELLER 1:

Where swinging wide at her moorings lay
The Somerset, **British man-of-war;**[5]

(SOUND CREW 5 shakes tambourine emphasizing the menace of the ship.)

STORYTELLER 1:

A phantom ship, with each mast and spar[6]
Across the MOON like a prison bar,
And a huge black hulk that was magnified
By its own reflection in the tide.

(SOMERSET steps right hiding under fabric to resemble "black hulk" as SOUND CREW 3 and 4 shake maracas and SOUND CREW 6 scrapes guiro. Finally, SOUND CREW 1 strikes triangle five times to end the scene.)

SCENE TWO

Characters: Four storytellers, Friend, Muster of Men (3 or more), Pigeon (1 or more), Moonlight, Bridge of Boats (3 or more)

STORYTELLER 2:

Meanwhile his FRIEND through alley and street,
Wanders and watches with eager ears,

(FRIEND *paces back and forth downstage shading eyes and looking over audience as SOUND CREW 6 strikes guiro.)*

STORYTELLER 2:

Till in the silence around him he hears
A muster[7] **of British at their barrack door**

(On "Muster," GRENADIERS, led by CAPTAIN, stand, salute, and freeze.)

STORYTELLER 2:

The sound of arms, and the tramp of feet,
And the measured tread of the grenadiers,[8]
Marching down to their boats on the shore.

(SOUND CREW 3 *strikes drum lightly as the* GRENADIERS *led by* CAPTAIN *march "in place" after "tramp of feet."*)

STORYTELLER 3:

Then he climbed the tower of the Old North Church.
By the wooden stairs, with stealthy tread,
To the belfry-chamber overhead,

(FRIEND, holding two lanterns, climbs ladder as SOUND CREW 2 strikes guiro for climbing.)

STORYTELLER 3:

And startled the PIGEONS from their perch
On the sombre rafters,[9] that round him made
Masses and moving shapes of shade—

(SOUND CREW 5 shakes tambourine as PIGEONS form on each side of ladder and move hands to create "startled.")

STORYTELLER 3:

By the trembling ladder, steep and tall,
To the highest window in the wall,
Where he paused to listen and look down
A moment on the roofs of the town,
And the moonlight flowing over all.

(FRIEND looks over audience and Boston. ROOFS form line across Boston. MOON stands center and MOONLIGHT ripples over ROOFS as SOUND CREW 5 shakes tambourine.)

STORYTELLER 4:

A moment only he froze under the spell
Of the place and the hour, and the secret dread
Of the lonely belfry and the dead;

(SOUND CREW 1 strikes triangle three times.)

STORYTELLER 1:

For suddenly all his thoughts are bent
On a shadowy something far away,
Where the river widens to meet the bay—
A line of black that bends and floats
Of the rising tide, like a bridge of boats.

(SOUND CREW 3 and 4 shake rattles as BOATS form line in river up left and freeze. FRIEND freezes too as SOUND CREW 1 strikes triangle five times for transition between scenes.)

SCENE 3

Characters: Four Storytellers, Revere, Horse, Friend, Spark, Moonlight

STORYTELLER 2:

Meanwhile, impatient to mount and ride,
Booted and spurred, with a heavy stride
On the opposite shore walked Paul Revere.

(REVERE paces on Charlestown side as SOUND CREW 6 strikes guiro for pacing.)

STORYTELLER 2:

Now he patted his horse's side,

(HORSE steps up right. REVERE pats horse as SOUND CREW 6 shakes jingle bells lightly.)

STORYTELLER 3:

Now gazed at the landscape far and near,

(SOUND CREW 1 strikes triangle three times for gazing.)

STORYTELLER 3:

Then, impetuous, stamped the earth,
And turned and tightened his saddle-girth;[10]

(REVERE stamps twice as SOUND CREW 2 strikes wood block twice. SOUND CREW 3 and 4 shake maracas lightly as REVERE tightens girth.)

STORYTELLER 3:

But mostly he watched with eager search
The belfry-tower of the Old North Church,

(SOUND CREW 1 strikes triangle three times after "church.")

STORYTELLER 3:

As it rose above the graves on the hill,
Lonely and spectral and sombre and still.

(SOUND CREW 5 shakes tambourine evoking mystery.)

STORYTELLER 4:

And lo! as he looks, on the belfry's height
A glimmer, and then a gleam of light!

(SOUND CREW 5 shakes tambourine on "glimmer." SOUND CREW 1 strikes triangle on "light" as REVERE shading eyes looks toward belfry and FRIEND holds up one lantern.)

STORYTELLER 4:

He springs to the saddle, the bridle he turns,

(SOUND CREW 5 shakes tambourine on "springs," as REVERE mimes above actions.)

STORYTELLER 4:

But lingers and gazes, till full on his sight
A SECOND lamp in the belfry burns!

(SOUND CREW 1 strikes triangle twice as REVERE continues looking up and FRIEND holds second lantern.)

STORYTELLER 1:

A hurry of hoofs in a village street,

(SOUND CREW 2 strikes wood block as REVERE gallops a short distance across Charlestown area and then stops and "in place" mimes a gallop, perhaps with feet stationary.)

STORYTELLER 1:

A shape in the moonlight, a bulk in the dark,
And beneath from the pebbles, in passing, a spark

(SOUND CREW 2 continues striking wood block as REVERE continues "in place" gallop. SOUND CREW 6 strikes guiro twice as SPARK flashes by HORSE'S hooves.)

STORYTELLER 2:

That was all! And yet, through the gloom and the light
The fate of a nation was riding that night;

(SOUND CREW 2 continues striking wood block as REVERE continues "in place" gallop.)

STORYTELLER 2:

And the spark struck out by that steed[11] in his flight.
Kindled the land into flame with its heat.

(SOUND CREW 6 strikes guiro on "spark." Sound CREW 5 shakes tambourine as SPARK kindles into flame. REVERE and HORSE freeze in gallop stance as SOUND CREW 1 strikes triangle five times as transition between scenes.)

SCENE FOUR

Characters: Four Storytellers, Revere, Medford Sign Holder, Cock, Dog, Fog, Lexington Sign Holder, Weathercock, Meeting-house Windows

STORYTELLER 3:

It was TWELVE by the village clock,
When he crossed the bridge into MEDFORD[12] town.

(SOUND CREW 4 strikes gong twelve times as MEDFORD SIGN HOLDER holds sign. Note: After REVERE gallops to each destination, he freezes in "gallop stance" waiting for narration to gallop to the next place.)

STORYTELLER 3:

He heard the crowing of the COCK,
And the barking of the farmer's DOG,

(COCK crows and DOG barks twice urging Revere on.)

STORYTELLER 3:

And felt the damp of the RIVER FOG,
That rises after the sun goes down.

(FOG flutters and spreads over river as SOUND CREW 5 shakes tambourine.)

STORYTELLER 4:

It was ONE by the village clock
When he galloped into Lexington.[13]

(SOUND CREW 4 strikes gong once as LEXINGTON SIGN HOLDER holds up sign.)

STORYTELLER 4:

He saw the gilded WEATHERCOCK[14]
Swim in the MOONLIGHT as he passed,

(WEATHERCOCK sways in front of MOON and MOONLIGHT as SOUND CREW 6 shakes jingle bells.)

STORYTELLER 4:

And the meeting-house windows, blank and bare,
Gaze at him with a spectral[15] **glare,**
As if they already stood aghast
At the bloody work they would look upon.

(SOUND CREW 3 and 4 shake maracas as MEETING-HOUSE WINDOWS create windows with arms. They stare ahead, and freeze. SOUND CREW 1 strikes triangle five times.)

SCENE FIVE

Characters: Four Storytellers, Revere, Concord Sign Holder, Flock, Birds (2 or more), Morning breeze, One safe in bed

STORYTELLER 1:

It was two by the village clock,
When he came to the bridge in Concord[16] **Town.**

(SOUND CREW 5 strikes gong twice as CONCORD SIGNHOLDER takes position.)

STORYTELLER 1:
He heard the bleating of the flock,

(FLOCK bleats lightly.)

STORYTELLER 1:
And the twitter of birds among the trees,

(BIRDS twitter.)

STORYTELLER 1:
And felt the breath on the morning breeze
Blowing over the meadows brown.

(SOUND CREW 3 and 4 shakes maracas as MORNING BREEZE ripples fabric above REVERE.)

STORYTELLER 2:
And one was safe and asleep in his bed
Who at the bridge would be first to fall,
Who that day would be lying dead,
Pierced by a British musket-ball.

STORYTELLER 3:
You know the rest, in the books you have read,
How the British regulars[17] fired and fled—

(SOUND CREW 6 strikes wood block several times rapidly after "fired" and SOUND CREW 5 shakes tambourine and then slaps it in the center after "fled.")

STORYTELLER 4:
So through the night rode Paul Revere;

(SOUND CREW 2 strikes wood block as REVERE faces audience galloping "in place.")

STORYTELLER 4:

A voice in the darkness, a knock at the door,
And a word that shall echo for evermore!

STORYTELLER 1:

In the hour of darkness and peril and need,
The people will waken and listen to hear
The hurrying hoofbeats of that steed,
And the midnight message of Paul Revere.

CHORUS *(Standing and led by STORYTELLER 1.)*

In the hour of darkness and peril and need,
The people will waken and listen to hear
The hurrying hoofbeats of that steed,
And the midnight message of Paul Revere.

(CHORUS remains standing and gestures toward REVERE and HORSE and freeze. REVERE and HORSE stand center stage facing stage left in gallop stance as SOUND CREW 1 strikes triangle five times to end the drama.)

THE END

NOTES:

1 belfry arch: The curved top of a tower or steeple that holds the bells
2 Charlestown: Part of Boston on the harbor
3 Middlesex: A county in Massachusetts
4 muffled: Wrapped in material to deaden sound
5 man-of-war: An armed naval ship; warship
6 mast and spar: Poles to support sails
7 muster: Roll call or an assembly of military troops summoned for inspection
8 grenadiers: Members of a special regiment or corps
9 rafters: The beams that slope from ridge of a roof to support the roof
10 girth: Band around the belly of a horse to hold a saddle
11 steed: Horse, especially a high-spirited riding horse
12 Medford: A town outside of Boston
13 Lexington: A town outside of Boston.
14 weathercock: A weathervane in the form or a rooster
15 spectral: Ghostly
16 Concord: A town in eastern Massachusetts. The first battles of the American Revolutionary War were fought in Lexington and Concord.
17 British Regulars: Members of the army of Great Britain

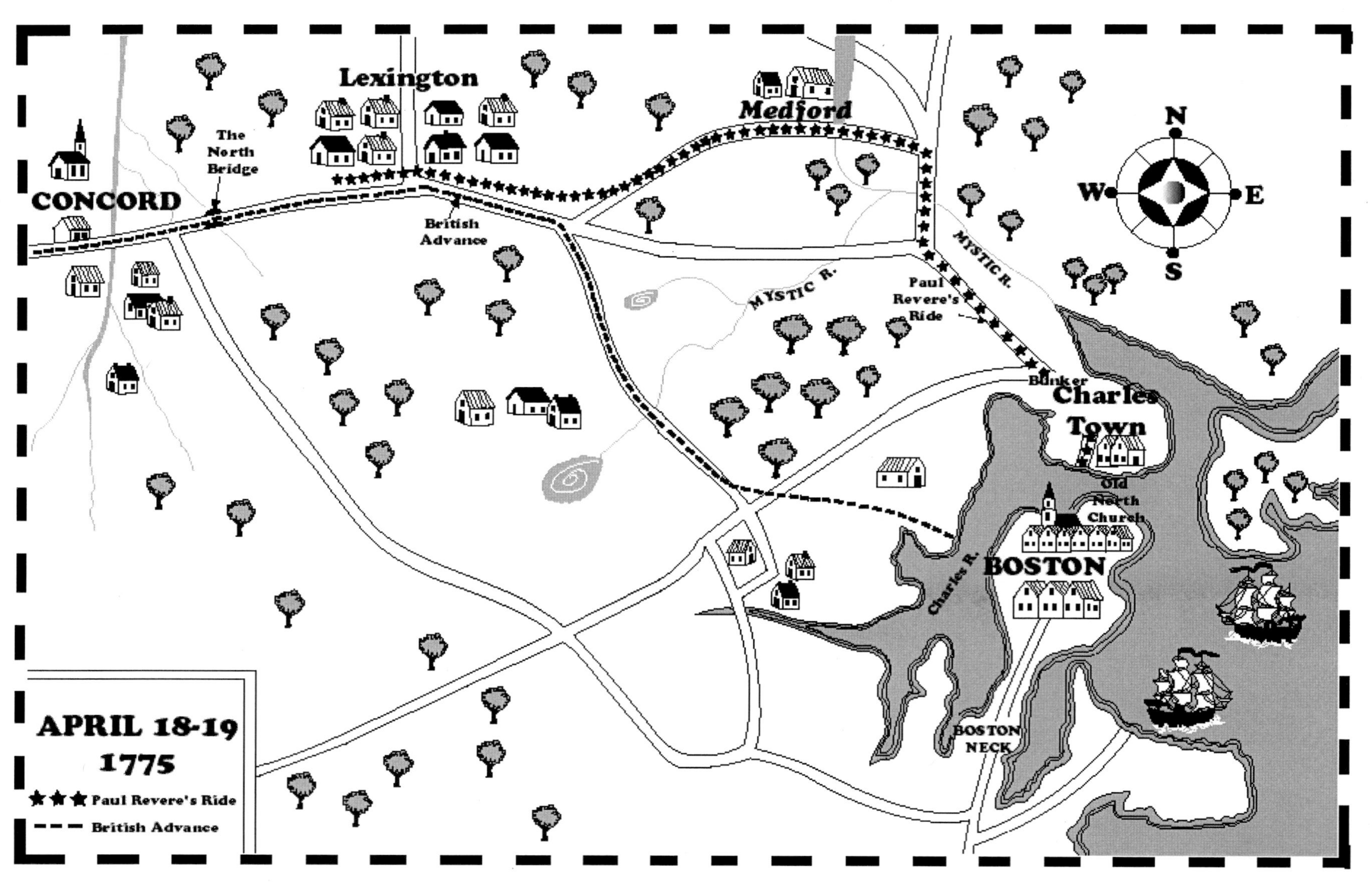
N
E
S
W
CONCORD
The North Bridge
Lexington
British Advance
Medford
MYSTIC R.
Paul Revere's Ride
Bunker
Charles Town
Old North Church
BOSTON
Charles R.
BOSTON NECK
APRIL 18-19
1775
Paul Revere's Ride
British Advance

COSTUME AND PROP SUGGESTIONS: For poetry dramatization presentations, all students wear black shirts and black pants with individual character costumes pieces added to the all-black attire. The costumes should be simple and make a clear statement. STORYTELLERS might wear tunics of red, white, and blue or tri-cornered hats.

Storytellers: Choir robes or tunics in patriotic colors
April 18, 1875 Sign Holder: Tagboard sign approximately 9 by 12 inches with date written on it
Paul Revere: Tri-cornered black hat with silver trim
His Friend: Similar hat, not trimmed
North Church Sign Holder: Tagboard sign with written on it or use a ladder (labeled North Church)
Paul Revere's Boat: Office chair with wheels
Charlestown Sign Holder: Tagboard sign with Charleston written on it
Charles River: Two pieces of filmy blue fabric wiggled to create river
Moon: Cardboard crescent moon covered with aluminum foil
Moonlight: Silver tinsel attached to two dowels
The Somerset British Man-of-War ship: Light weight black fabric to create "black hulk"
Marching Grenadiers: No costume other than black clothing is necessary.
Captain of Grenadiers: Captain-style tall hat
Lanterns: Two flashlights
Pigeons: White or light gray gloves
Bridge of British boats: No costume other than black clothing is necessary.
Paul's horse: Black ribbon or yarn to create mane attached to top of a black baseball cap. Add black ears.
Spark (kindling into flame): Gold tinsel attached to two dowels
Medford sign holder: Tagboard sign with Medford written on it
Cock: Vocalized sound effect only
Dog: Sound effect only
Fog: White nylon netting or dowels with white crepe paper strips
Lexington sign holder: Tagboard sign with Lexington written on it
Gilded Weathercock: Tagboard weathercock spray painted gold and put on a ruler or dowel
Meeting-house windows: No costume other than black clothing is necessary.
Flock of sheep: Vocalized sound effect only
Concord sign holder: Tagboard sign with Concord written on it
Twittering birds: Sound effect only

TOPICS FOR CRITICAL THINKING, WRITING, AND ART

1. *Paul Revere's Ride* is not completely factually correct. Is it still a good poem? Explain your answer.

2. Research the life of Paul Revere and do a television interview with him. Ask: How did you get into this situation? What was the most exciting or difficult part of it? What are your plans for the future?

3. *Paul Revere's Ride* describes an important heroic American event. Do you think people of other countries would enjoy the poem too? Explain.

4. In the poem, the Americans outwit the British. What do you think a British person's attitude might be toward the poem? Explain.

5. What does Revere do in the poem that shows he's resourceful and clever?

6. Why do you think many people consider Paul Revere a hero? What does he do that makes him a hero?

7. For almost one hundred years after Paul Revere's ride in 1775 not many people had heard of the ride and it was just one event leading to the American Revolutionary War. Why do you think the poem written in 1861 made the event famous?

8. This poem is in a meter called anapestic tetrameter, that creates a rhythm

of galloping. Recite the beginning of the poem and experience the galloping rhythm. Why is this rhythm appropriate for the poem?

9. *Paul Revere's Ride* is an action poem. Find a stanza that demonstrates or shows action.

10. Readers have said that *Paul Revere's Ride* is exciting both for its action and the suspenseful, eerie mood it creates. Find stanzas in the poem that create suspense and the spooky mood.

11. A narrative poem is like a short story. It has a setting, plot, characters, dialogue, and a theme. Where does Paul Revere's Ride take place? What is the plot? Who are the central characters? Which characters speak? What is the main idea?

12. USING THE MAP: Find the North Church where the signal was given. Find the three towns referred to in the poem. Using the map key, trace the route that Paul Revere and Dr. Prescott (another rider in the relay) took to warn the people the British were coming. Trace the route the British took.

ART: Find something in *Paul Revere's Ride* that you feel is a good symbol of some aspect of the poem, such as the tower with the two lanterns or Paul Revere on his horse in the moonlight. Draw a picture of your symbol and write about why you chose it.

CHAPTER FOURTEEN

A Poetry Performance

All the world's a stage,
And all the men and women merely players:
—William Shakespeare, *As You Like It,* Act II, Sc. 7

PRODUCING THIS POETRY PERFORMANCE

The following is a poetry performance of about 25 minutes. It includes nonsense verse, limericks, nature lyrics, animal poetry, and a patriotic finale, "America the Beautiful." The script includes gestures and rhythm instruments to play for each line of a poem. Suggested costume pieces for all poems are at the end of the script.

STORYTELLERS introduce the poems. They use scripts to follow the sequence.

ACTORS are assigned numbers indicating lines to recite. Their lines are short and should be memorized.

The CHORUS consists of all participants, except SOUND CREW; it includes ACTORS when they are not acting individual roles or reciting. In some poems the CHORUS will stand in place and perform gestures as individual actors step forward and perform. In other poems, the CHORUS will remain seated—sometimes acting and sometimes not. The script indicates when they act.

The SOUND CREW sit at long tables with their rhythm instruments. See diagram that follows.

For more tips on producing and directing a poetry performance, see Chapter Four, Directing a Poetry Performance. For suggestions on creating your own poetry performance script, see Chapter Eight, Choosing and Adapting Poems to Dramatize.

SOUND CREW

Sound Crew 1 Triangle
Sound Crew 2 Wood block
Sound Crew 3 Maraca (or rattle), drum
Sound Crew 4 Maraca (or rattle), jingle bells
Sound Crew 5 Tambourine, bike horn
Sound Crew 6 Tape recorder, guiro, jingle bells, tone bells or piano

BASIC STAGE SETUP

The actors sit in chairs arranged in a semicircle in view of the audience. Costumes and props are stored under the actors' chairs; they are put on and taken off when needed.

The Sound Crew sits with instruments on a table to the right of the stage area, in view of the audience. The tables are set so that the Crew can see the stage.

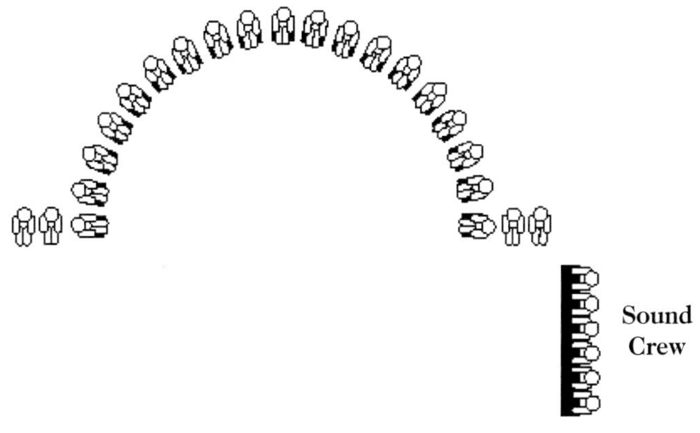

CAST OF CHARACTERS

Storyteller 1 (Leader; very responsible, strong energy and voice)
Storytellers 2, 3, 4 (Also energetic with strong voices; ability to follow and pick up cues)
Chorus (All participants not in selected roles)

SCENE ONE: Nonsense Verse

Chorus (All participants not in selected roles)
Humpty Dumpty: Humpty Dumpty
Jack Be Nimble: Jack
Rub-A-Dub-Dub: (3) Butcher, Baker, Candlestick Maker
Old Mother Hubbard: (2) Old Mother Hubbard, Dog
Oh, The Grand Old Duke of York: Duke of York

SCENE TWO: Limericks

A Piggish Young Person from Leeds: Piggish Person

There Was an Old Man from Peru: Old Man

An Epicure Dining at Crewe: (2) Epicure, Waiter

Higglety, Pigglety, Pop!: (3) Dog, Pig, Cat

A Wiggling Mouse Woke Miss Dowd: (2) Miss Dowd, Mouse

There Was a Young Lady of Niger: (2) Lady, Tiger

A Flea and a Fly in a Flue: (4) Flea, Fly, (2) Flue

SCENE THREE: Nature Poems

Chorus (All participants not in selected roles)

Windy Nights: (2) Man (Man of style and mystery), Horse (Graceful prancer)

The Wind: (2) Actor-Reciters

Raindrops: (6)People

Silver: (5) Moon (graceful with balletlike movements), Dog (perky) Mouse (nimble), Two Doves (light and airy). The Chorus gestures as Trees, Casements, Thatch, Cotes, and Reeds as indicated in the script.

SCENE FOUR: Animal Poetry

Chorus sits (Chorus acts while seated as indicated in script.)

*How Creatures Move: (*7 or more) Lion, Squirrel, Flies, Seals, Worm, Monkey, Birds

The Ballad of Mister Fox: (7 or more) Mister Fox (tricky and agile) Moon, Duck, Goose, Mrs. Slipper Slopper (very nervous), John (ready for action), Mrs. Fox (very hungry), The Little Foxes (very, very hungry)

The Eagle: (6) Eagle (proud, powerful), Crag, Sun, Azure World, Sea (2)

SCENE FIVE: America the Beautiful Finale

Chorus

America the Beautiful (10), Sky (2), Grain (2), Purple Mountains (2), Fruited Plain, Crowned Good (Statue of Liberty), Flag Wavers (2)

USE OF THE TRIANGLE

1. AT THE BEGINNING OF EACH SCENE of poems, Sound Crew 1 strikes the triangle three times to signal that a new Scene will be performed and as a transition between the scenes or types of poems. The signal also tells actors to put on costumes for the poems in the next scene.

2. AT THE BEGINNING OF EACH POEM, Sound Crew 1 strikes the triangle after the title and author (if known) to accentuate them and to signal actors to take their positions on stage and freeze so they are ready to perform.

3. AT THE END OF EACH POEM, the actors freeze after the final line creating a frozen picture of the final line. Then, Sound Crew 1 counts silently to five and strikes the triangle as a release signaling actors to return to their seats and to be ready to act the next poem.

PERFORMANCE OPENING

SOUND CREW 6 plays taped Mozart's Eine Kleine Nacht Musik *or some other light classical music to set a happy, bright classic mood.*

Then, SOUND CREW 1 strikes the triangle slowly three times to signal the performance will begin. STORYTELLERS rise on the third strike of the triangle, and STORYTELLER 1 speaks immediately using high energy and strong projection to grab the audience's attention. CHORUS remains seated.

STORYTELLER 1: *(Energetically, waving.)* Welcome, students, adults too.
STORYTELLER 2: *(Pointing at audience on "you.")* Today we'll do a show for you.
STORYTELLER 3: *(Raising hands up on "new.")* Of classic poems, old, yet new.
STORYTELLER 4: *(Opening arms up colorfully.)* We'll make them come alive for you.
STORYTELLER 1: *(Pointing enthusiastically.)* So, sit right here and have some fun.
STORYTELLER 2: *(Gesturing toward heart.)* We hope you like them everyone.
STORYTELLER 3: Now to set our imaginations free.
STORYTELLER 4: We'll act some NONSENSE full of glee.
STORYTELLER 1 We like their rhythm. We like their rhyme.
STORYTELLER 2: They always offer a real good time.

SCENE ONE: NONSENSE VERSE

SOUND CREW 1 strikes the triangle three times. All the actors (THE CHORUS) stand in front of their chairs to both recite and act all of the Nonsense Verse. The CHORUS remains standing until all Nonsense Verse is completed. The STORYTELLER announcing the rhyme leads the CHORUS in the recitation and actions.

ACTORS performing characters in individual poems step center stage to act their parts and then rejoin the CHORUS.

STORYTELLER 1:
Humpty Dumpty by Mother Goose

(SOUND CREW 1 strikes triangle. CHORUS stands and HUMPTY wobbles center. SOUND CREW 3 strikes drum to accompany HUMPTY.)

STORYTELLER 1, HUMPTY AND CHORUS:
Humpty Dumpty sat on a wall,

(SOUND CREW 3 strikes drum. HUMPTY and CHORUS make big stomachs and wobble.)

STORYTELLER 1, HUMPTY AND CHORUS:
Humpty Dumpty had a great fall.

(SOUND CREW 3 strikes gong as HUMPTY and CHORUS fall slowly.)

STORYTELLER 1, HUMPTY AND CHORUS:
All the king's horses and all the king's men,

(SOUND CREW 2 strikes wood block. CHORUS stoops and slaps knees rhythmically.)

STORYTELLER 1, HUMPTY AND CHORUS:
Couldn't put Humpty together again.

(SOUND CREW 5 shakes tambourine as the KING'S MEN-CHORUS shake heads, shrug, and freeze. SOUND CREW 1 strikes triangle. HUMPTY wobbles to seat as SOUND CREW 3 strikes drum.)

STORYTELLER 2:
Jack Be Nimble by Mother Goose

(SOUND CREW 1 strikes triangle. JACK skips center SOUND CREW 6 shakes jingle bells.)

STORYTELLER 2:
Jack be nimble,

(SOUND CREW 4 and 6 shake jingle bells. JACK and CHORUS spin.)

STORYTELLER 2:
Jack be quick,

(SOUND CREW 2 strikes wood block as JACK and CHORUS run knees high "in place.")

STORYTELLER 2:
Jack jump over

(SOUND CREW 6 strikes wood block as JACK and CHORUS leap with outstretched arms.)

STORYTELLER 2:
The candlestick.

(SOUND CREW 6 shakes jingle bells. Jack and CHORUS point to imaginary candlestick. CHORUS's hands become shimmering candle flame and freeze. SOUND CREW 1 strikes triangle, and Jack skips to seat as SOUND CREW 4 and 6 shake bells.)

STORYTELLER 3:
Rub-a-Dub-Dub by Mother Goose

(SOUND CREW 1 strikes triangle. The three men hands on hips strut center as SOUND CREW 5 shakes tambourine.)

STORYTELLER 3:
Rub-a-dub-dub

(SOUND CREW 3 and 4 shake maracas. MEN and CHORUS swivel hips vigorously side to side.)

STORYTELLER 3:
Three men in a tub

(SOUND CREW 2 strikes wood block as MEN and CHORUS thrust three fingers and heads in and out.)

STORYTELLER 3:
And who do you think they be?

(SOUND CREW 3 and 4 shakes maracas as MEN shrug rhythmically.)

STORYTELLER 3:
The butcher,

(SOUND CREW 6 scrapes guiro as BUTCHER and CHORUS jump forward holding imaginary knife.)

STORYTELLER 3:
The baker,

(SOUND CREW 4 shake maracas as BAKER and CHORUS jump forward and stir in huge bowl.)

STORYTELLER 3:
The candlestick maker.

(SOUND CREW 2 strikes wood block as CANDLESTICK MAKER and CHORUS jump forward holding stick.)

STORYTELLER 3:
Toss 'em out, knaves all three.

(SOUND CREW 3 and 4 shake maracas vigorously as MEN and CHORUS fall overboard holding noses, "Glub, glub!" SOUND CREW 1 strikes triangle. SOUND CREW 5 shakes tambourine. Men sit.)

STORYTELLER 4:
Old Mother Hubbard by Mother Goose

(SOUND CREW 1 strikes triangle. MOTHER HUBBARD and the CHORUS hobble and the DOG skips center as SOUND CREW 2 strikes wood block.)

STORYTELLER 4:
Old Mother Hubbard

(SOUND CREW 3 and 4 shake maracas as MOTHER HUBBARD and CHORUS shake holding cane.)

STORYTELLER 4.
Went to the cupboard,

(SOUND CREW 2 strikes wood block as MOTHER HUBBARD and CHORUS hobble and reach up showing cupboard.)

STORYTELLER 4:
To fetch her poor dog a bone.

(DOG, paws up, barks excitedly "WOOF! WOOF!")

STORYTELLER 4:
But when she got there

(SOUND CREW 2 strikes wood block as MOTHER HUBBARD and CHORUS hobbles and stops.)

STORYTELLER 4:
The cupboard was bare,

(SOUND CREW 2 strikes triangle. *MOTHER HUBBARD and CHORUS open cupboard, eyes and arms wide.)*

STORYTELLER 4:
And so the poor dog had none.

(SOUND CREW 2 strikes wood block twice as DOG and CHORUS woof pathetically and MOTHER HUBBARD shaking head sadly says, "Poor doggie," and freezes. SOUND CREW 1 strikes triangle. SOUND CREW 2 strikes wood block as MOTHER HUBBARD hobbles and DOG skips to seats.)

STORYTELLER 1:
Oh, the Grand Old Duke of York by Mother Goose

(SOUND CREW 1 strikes triangle. Duke marches center pompously—knees high and chest out as SOUND CREW 3 strikes drum.)

STORYTELLER 1:
Oh, the grand old Duke of York,

(SOUND CREW 3 strikes drum rhythmically as DUKE and CHORUS march "in place" and salute.)

STORYTELLER 1:
He had ten thousand men;

(SOUND CREW 3 strikes drum as DUKE thrusts ten fingers in and out rhythmically.)

STORYTELLER 1:
He marched them to the top of the hill,

(SOUND CREW 3 strikes drum in marching rhythm as DUKE and CHORUS march "in place" swinging arms high.)

STORYTELLER 1:
And he marched them down again.

(SOUND CREW 3 strikes drum as DUKE and CHORUS march, stooping and swinging arms low.)

STORYTELLER 1:
And when they were up, they were up,

(SOUND CREW 3 strikes drum as DUKE and CHORUS raise arms up.)

STORYTELLER 1:
And when they were down, they were down,

(SOUND CREW 3 strikes drum as DUKE and CHORUS stoop.)

STORYTELLER 1:
And when they were only halfway up,

(SOUND CREW 3 strikes drum as DUKE and CHORUS rise halfway up.)

STORYTELLER 1:
They were neither up nor down.

(SOUND CREW 3 strikes drum as DUKE and CHORUS raise arms up and then stoop down. SOUND CREW 1 strikes triangle. SOUND CREW 3 strikes drum firmly to accompany Duke marching pompously to seat. SOUND CREW 1 strikes triangle. CHORUS and ACTORS sit.)

(Actors put on costumes for Scene Two: Limericks. CHORUS doesn't act in the Limericks and remains sitting throughout the Limericks.)

SCENE TWO: LIMERICKS

SOUND CREW 1 strikes the triangle three times.

STORYTELLER 2:
LIMERICKS are lively and quick.
They come from the place, Limerick.
Each verse has five lines,
And all of them rhyme,
And the RHYMING is quite a slick TRICK.

STORYTELLER 3:
A Piggish Young Person from Leeds

(SOUND CREW 1 strikes triangle. SOUND CREW 3 and 4 shake maracas as PIGGISH PERSON smacking lips and rubbing hands greedily strides center.)

STORYTELLER 3:
A piggish young person from Leeds

(SOUND CREW 3 and 4 shake rattles as PERSON rubs hands greedily.)

STORYTELLER 3:
Made a meal on six packets of seeds

(SOUND CREW 2 strikes wood block six times as PERSON reaches up for each packet, opens each one and eats.)

STORYTELLER 3:
But it soon came to pass

(SOUND CREW 4 and 6 shake jingle bells as PERSON opens up arms.)

STORYTELLER 3:
That he broke out in grass

(SOUND CREW 3 and 4 shake rattles as PERSON brushes weeds off legs.)

STORYTELLER 3:
And he couldn't sit down for the weeds.
PERSON: *(Turning sideways and rubbing rear end)*
OW!

(SOUND CREW 5 shakes tambourine and slaps it in the center. SOUND CREW 1 strikes triangle. SOUND CREW 3 and 4 shake rattles as PIGGISH PERSON rubbing rear end sits.)

STORYTELLER 4:
There Was an Old Man from Peru

(SOUND CREW 1 strikes triangle. SOUND CREW 2 strikes wood block. Old Man bent over, holding and shaking pipe and imaginary cane hobbles center.)

STORYTELLER 4:
There was an old man from Peru

(SOUND CREW 6 shakes jingle bells. MAN shaking cane, bows.)

STORYTELLER 4:
Who dreamed he was eating his shoe.

(SOUND CREW 3 and 4 shake maracas as MAN lying down chomps shoe.)

STORYTELLER 4:
In the midst of the night
He awoke in a fright

(SOUND CREW 2 strikes wood block. MAN throws arms up and opens eyes wide.)

STORYTELLER 4:
And—good grief, it was perfectly true!
OLD MAN: *(Examining shoe.)*
OH, NO!

(SOUND CREW 5 shakes tambourine and slaps it in center as MAN examines shoe, "OH, NO!" SOUND CREW 1 strikes triangle. SOUND CREW 2 strikes wood block as OLD MAN hobbling and scratching head sits.)

STORYTELLER 1:
An Epicure Dining at Crewe

(SOUND CREW 1 strikes triangle. SOUND CREW 2 strikes wood block as

EPICURE nose in air struts center followed by bossy WAITER with hands on hips.)

STORYTELLER 1:
An epicure, dining at Crewe,

(SOUND CREW 3 and 4 shake maracas as EPICURE eats fussily.)

STORYTELLER 1:
Found quite a large mouse in his (her) stew.

(SOUND CREW 1 strikes triangle. EPICURE indignantly raises mouse high.)

STORYTELLER 1:
Said the waiter,
WAITER: *(Pointing at EPICURE.)*
"Don't shout, and wave it about,

(SOUND CREW 4 shakes tambourine as glaring WAITER leans forward wagging finger at diner.)

WAITER: *(Gesturing to the audience, the other diners.)*
Or the rest will be wanting one, too!"

(SOUND CREW 5 shakes tambourine and slaps it in the center as WAITER hands on hips glares at EPICURE. SOUND CREW 1 strikes triangle. SOUND CREW 2 strikes wood block as EPICURE disgustedly holds mouse high as he returns to his seat followed by irritated WAITER hands on hips.)

STORYTELLER 2:
Higglety, Pigglety, Pop! by Samuel Goodrich

(SOUND CREW 1 strikes triangle. SOUND CREW 4 and 6 shake bells. DOG, PIG, AND CAT skip center.)

STORYTELLER 2:
Higglety, pigglety, pop!

(SOUND CREW 5 shakes tambourine and slaps it in center as DOG, PIG, and CAT spin to the left on "Higglety," to the right on "Pigglety" and hop up on "Pop!")

STORYTELLER 2:
The dog has eaten the mop;

(SOUND CREW 6 scrapes guiro. DOG eats mop gnawing up and down handle, "Woof! Woof!")

STORYTELLER 2:
The pig's in a hurry,

(SOUND CREW 3 and 4 shake maracas. PIG runs hoofs high rapidly "in place," "Oink, oink.")

STORYTELLER 2:
The cat's in a flurry,

(SOUND CREW 6 shakes jingle bells. CAT waves paws wildly, "Meow, meow.")

STORYTELLER 2:
Higglety, pigglety, POP!

(ALL repeat first action and freeze with arms up. SOUND CREW 5 shakes tambourine and slaps in center. SOUND CREW 1 strikes triangle. SOUND CREW 4 and 6 shake jingle bells as DOG, PIG, AND CAT skip to chairs and sit.)

STORYTELLER 3 :
Miss Dowd and the Mouse, adapted by Lousie Thistle

(SOUND CREW 1 strikes triangle. SOUND CREW 2 strikes wood block as no-nonsense MISS DOWD strides and wiggling MOUSE scurries center.)

STORYTELLER 3:
A wiggling mouse woke Miss Dowd.

(SOUND CREW 3 and 4 shake maracas. MOUSE wiggles. MISS DOWD opens eyes and arms wide in alarm.)

STORYTELLER 3:
She jumped up and yelled very loud.

(SOUND CREW 2 strikes wood block twice as MISS DOWD yells, "EEEEK, EEEEK!"

STORYTELLER 3:
Then a happy thought hit her:

(SOUND CREW 2 strikes wood block as DOWD touches head.)

STORYTELLER 3:
To scare off the critter,

(MISS DOWD stretches arms forward as if cat on attack.)

STORYTELLER 3:
She stood on her bed and meowed.
MISS DOWD:
M-E-O-O-O-W W!

(SOUND CREW 5 shakes tambourine and slaps in center. SOUND CREW 5 shakes tambourine vigorously. SOUND CREW 1 strikes triangle. SOUND CREW 2 strikes wood block as glaring MISS DOWD and trembling MOUSE sit.)

STORYTELLER 4:
There Was a Young Lady of Niger

(SOUND CREW 1 strikes triangle. SOUND CREW 4 and 6 shake bells as LADY smiling and fanning self and TIGER pawing go center.)

STORYTELLER 4:
There was a young lady of Niger

(SOUND CREW 6 shakes jingle bells as smiling LADY curtsies, fanning self.)

STORYTELLER 4:
Who smiled as she rode on a tiger.

(SOUND CREW 3 and 4 shake maracas as smiling LADY fanning walks behind TIGER who strides across stage.)

STORYTELLER 4:
They returned from the ride

(LADY and TIGER walk across stage in opposite direction with LADY behind TIGER.)

STORYTELLER 4:
With the lady inside

(SOUND CREW 3 strikes drum as LADY stoops behind TIGER who spreads out tunic to conceal her.)

STORYTELLER 4:
And the smile on the face of the tiger.

(SOUND CREW 5 shakes tambourine and slaps it in center as TIGER licks lips, "YUM, YUM." SOUND CREW 1 strikes triangle. SOUND CREW 3 and 4 shake bells as TIGER striding and LADY fanning herself go to their seats.)

STORYTELLER 1:
A Flea and a Fly in a Flue

(SOUND CREW 1 strikes triangle. SOUND CREW 3 and 4 shake maracas as FLEA hopping and FLY flying stand visible to the audience on opposite sides of FLUE cloth that forms center.)

STORYTELLER 1:
A flea and a fly in a flue

(SOUND CREW 2 strikes wood block as FLEA and FLY go behind FLUE cloth held waist high so they can be seen behind it.)

STORYTELLER 1:
Were imprisoned, so what could they do?

(SOUND CREW 6 scrapes guiro. FLEA shrugs and hops and FLY shrugs and flaps wings.)

STORYTELLER 1:
Said the fly,
FLY:
"Let us flee."

(SOUND CREW 6 shakes jingle bells as FLY points up.)

STORYTELLER 1:
Said the flea,

FLEA:
"Let us fly,"

(SOUND CREW 3 and 4 shake maracas as FLEA flies in place.)

FLY and FLEA:
So they flew through a flaw in the flue.

(SOUND CREW 5 shakes tambourine and slaps in center as FLEA and FLY fly out from under FLUE cloth and freeze in triumph. SOUND CREW 1 strikes triangle. SOUND CREW 6 shakes jingle bells as FLEA hops, FLY flies, and FLUE moves briskly to seats. Actors put on costumes for Nature Poems.)

SCENE THREE: NATURE POEMS

SOUND CREW 1 strikes triangle three times to make transition between the poem types.

STORYTELLER 1:
Nature has rhythm. It's perfectly free.
STORYTELLER 2:
Nature moves poets. It also moves me.
STORYTELLER 3:
We now use movement and instruments too,
STORYTELLER 4:
To make the movement of nature come alive here for you.

(SOUND CREW 1 strikes triangle. CHORUS stands and remains standing throughout the Nature Poetry acting in all of these poems.)

STORYTELLER 3 :
Windy Nights
STORYTELLER 4:
By Robert Louis Stevenson

(SOUND CREW 1 strikes triangle.)
ACTOR 1:
Whenever the moon and stars are set,

(SOUND CREW 5 shakes tambourine. CHORUS wiggles fingers like twinkling stars and freeze.)

ACTOR 2:
Whenever the wind is high,

(SOUND CREW 3 and 4 shake maracas as CHORUS moves arms side to side saying, "SHHHH.")

ACTOR 3:
All night long in the dark and wet,

(SOUND CREW 2 strikes wood block lightly as CHORUS opens arms out to create a dark expanse.)

ACTOR 4:
A man goes riding by.

(SOUND CREW 2 strikes wood block rhythmically. CHORUS slaps knees as HORSE and MAN gallop in large circle around stage. MAN slaps his thighs urging HORSE on.)

ACTOR 5:
Late in the night when the fires are out,

(SOUND CREW 5 shakes tambourine as CHORUS shimmers fingers like fire. Then, hands disappear behind backs.)

ACTOR 6: *(Opening arms out in wonder.)*
Why does he gallop and gallop about?

(SOUND CREW 2 strikes wood block. CHORUS slaps knees. MAN and HORSE gallop.)

ACTOR 1:
Whenever the trees are crying aloud,

(SOUND CREW 5 shakes tambourine. CHORUS sways saying, "SHHHH.")

ACTOR 2:
And ships are tossed at sea,

(SOUND CREW 3 and 4 shake maracas. CHORUS's arms make tossing waves.)

ACTOR 3:
By, on the highway, low and loud,

(SOUND CREW 2 strikes wood block. CHORUS slaps knees. MAN and HORSE gallop to end.)

ACTOR 4:
By at the gallop goes he.
ACTOR 5:
By at the gallop he goes, and then
ACTOR 6:
By he comes back at the gallop again.

(MAN, leans forward freezing, urging HORSE on. HORSE freezes with one hoof raised in mid-prance position. Sound Crew 1 strikes triangle. MAN and HORSE rejoin CHORUS still standing.)

STORYTELLER 1:
The Wind

(SOUND CREW 1 strikes triangle.)

STORYTELLER 1:
By Christina Rossetti

(SOUND CREW 1 strikes triangle.)

ACTOR 7:
Who has seen the wind?

(SOUND CREW strikes triangle three times. ACTOR and CHORUS open arms out in wonder.)

ACTOR 7:
Neither I nor you;

(SOUND CREW 1 strikes triangle twice as ACTOR points to self and audience.)

ACTOR 7:
But when the leaves hang trembling

(SOUND CREW 6 shakes jingle bells. CHORUS and ACTOR'S fingers create trembling leaves.)

ACTOR 7:
The wind is passing through.

(SOUND CREW 5 shakes tambourine as 3 WIND ACTORS from each side of the stage lightly swirl across stage going to other WIND ACTORS places on opposite side.)

ACTOR 8:
Who has seen the wind?

(SOUND CREW 1 strikes triangle three times. CHORUS opens arms out in wonder.)

ACTOR 8:
Neither you nor I;

(SOUND CREW 1 strikes triangle twice as CHORUS points to audience and self.)

ACTOR 8:
But when the trees bow down their heads

(SOUND CREW 6 shakes jingle bells. CHORUS bows heads.)

ACTOR 8:
The wind is passing by.

(SOUND CREW 5 shakes tambourine lightly. WIND ACTORS swirl across to their original places. SOUND CREW 1 strikes triangle. ACTORS freeze. SOUND CREW 1 strikes triangle.)

STORYTELLER 3:
Raindrops

(SOUND CREW 1 strikes triangle.)

STORYTELLER 3:
By Anonymous, adapted by Louise Thistle

(SOUND CREW 1 strikes triangle.)

ACTOR 9:
Softly the rain goes pitter-patter,

(SOUND CREW 6 strikes two high piano notes or tone bell notes successively creating "pitter-patter" as CHORUS's fingers create falling rain.)

ACTOR 10:
Softly the rain comes falling down.

(SOUND CREW 6 strikes keys down scale of piano or tone bells from high to low as CHORUS's fingers create falling rain.)

ACTOR 11:
Hark to the people who hurry by:

(SOUND CREW 2 strikes wood block lightly as 3 PEOPLE walk briskly from one side of the stage to the other and back again, covering their heads or doing other actions to avoid rain.)

ACTOR 12:
Raindrops are teeny steps from the sky!

(SOUND CREW 2 strikes wood block lightly.)

ACTOR 13:
Softly the rain goes pitter-patter,

(SOUND CREW 6 strikes two high notes in succession as ACTOR'S fingers create falling rain.)

ACTOR 14:
Softly the rain comes falling down.

(SOUND CREW 6 strikes down scale of piano or tone bells from high to low as CHORUS's fingers create falling rain. SOUND CREW 1 strikes triangle. CHORUS remains standing.)

STORYTELLER 4:
Silver

(SOUND CREW 1 strikes triangle.)

STORYTELLER 4:
By Walter de la Mare

(SOUND CREW 1 strikes triangle.)

ACTOR 15:
Slowly, silently, now the moon

(SOUND CREW 1 strikes triangle three times as MOON majestically displaying tinsel in each hand walks in a gliding fashion to center.)

ACTOR 15:
Walks the night in her silver shoon;

(SOUND CREW 5 shakes tambourine. MOON walks slowly in serpentine pattern shimmering tinsel over every area of the stage.)

ACTOR 16:
This way, and that, she peers, and sees

(SOUND CREW 1 strikes triangle three times. MOON shades eyes and looks out over audience in all directions.)

ACTOR 16:
Silver fruit upon silver trees;

(SOUND CREW 6 shakes jingle bells. CHORUS arms create TREES. MOON shimmers tinsel over all of them.)

ACTOR 17:
One by one the casements catch
Her beams beneath the silvery thatch;

(CHORUS's arms create CASEMENTS. Then fingers make wiggling thatch as MOON shimmers tinsel over casements and thatch. SOUND CREW 5 shakes tambourine.)

ACTOR 18:

Couched in his kennel, like a log,
With paws of silver sleeps the dog;

(SOUND CREW 1 strikes wood block lightly. DOG bounces downstage left, kneels and sleeps paws by face, as MOON shimmers tinsel above him.)

ACTOR 19:

From their shadowy cote the white breasts peep
Of doves in a silver-feathered sleep;

(CHORUS's arms create COTES. SOUND CREW 1 strikes triangle lightly as DOVES fly to stage right and put wings across head and sleep as MOON shimmers tinsel above them.)

ACTOR 20:

A harvest mouse goes scampering by,
With silver claws, and silver eye;

(SOUND CREW 1 strikes wood block as MOUSE scurries downstage and freezes crouched with paws up. MOON shimmers tinsel on him.)

ACTOR 21:

And moveless fish in the waters gleam,

(SOUND CREW 3 and 4 shake maracas as CHORUS's hands and arms glide freezing up stage. MOON shimmers tinsel on them.)

ACTOR 21:

By silver reeds in a silver stream.

(SOUND CREW 6 shakes jingle bells as CHORUS's arms create swaying reeds. MOON shimmers tinsel. Then, all ACTORS create a frozen tableau.)
(SOUND CREW 1 strikes triangle. CHORUS and ACTORS sit.)

SCENE FOUR: ANIMAL POETRY

STORYTELLER 1:
Animal poems are great fun to act.
STORYTELLER 2:
Their movements make them perfect for that.
STORYTELLER 3:
Animals are agile and quite frisky too.
STORYTELLER 4:
We'll now act some animal poems for you.

(SOUND CREW 1 strikes triangle. CHORUS stands.)

STORYTELLER 4:
How Creatures Move

(SOUND CREW 1 strikes triangle.)

STORYTELLER 4:
By Anonymous, adapted by Louise Thistle

(SOUND CREW 1 strikes triangle.)

ACTOR 22:
The lion prowls on padded paws,

(SOUND CREW 3 strikes drum as LION paws mightily and freezes. CHORUS paws "in place" by chairs.)

ACTOR 23:
The squirrel leaps from limb to limb,

(SOUND CREW 1 strikes triangle. SQUIRREL leaps and freezes. CHORUS leaps "in place" by chairs.)

ACTOR 24:
While flies can crawl straight up a wall,

(SOUND CREW 2 strikes wood block. FLIES stoop, crawl up, and freeze. CHORUS crawls "in place" by chairs.)

ACTOR 25:

And seals can dive and swim.

(SOUND CREW 5 shakes tambourine. SEALS dive and swim and freeze. CHORUS dives and swims "in place" by chairs.)

ACTOR 26:

The worm wiggles his way around,

(SOUND CREW 6 scrapes guiro. WORM stoops, wiggles up and down, and freezes. CHORUS wiggles "in place" by chairs.)

ACTOR 27:

The monkey swings by his tail,

(SOUND CREW 3 and 4 shake maracas as MONKEY'S arms and body swings. CHORUS swings "in place" by chairs.)

ACTOR 28:

And birds may hop upon the ground,

(SOUND CREW 2 strikes wood block lightly as BIRDS hop. CHORUS hop "in place" by chairs.)

ACTOR 29:

Or spread their wings and sail.

(SOUND CREW 6 shake jingle bells as BIRDS fly and freeze on opposite sides of stage. CHORUS flies "in place" by chairs.)

ACTOR 30:

But people dancing have fun galore:

(SOUND CREW 3 and 4 shake maracas.)

ACTOR 31: *(Pausing to give ACTORS time to dance each "dance" word.):*

They twirl and twist and jive and soar.

(SOUND CREW 5 shakes tambourine and SOUND CREW 6 shakes bells. CHORUS and CREATURES as PEOPLE first twirl, then twist, jive, and finally soar freezing with arms soaring upwards. SOUND CREW 5 slaps tambourine in center. SOUND CREW 1 strikes triangle. CHORUS sits.)

STORYTELLER 1:
The Ballad of Mister Fox, adapted by Louise Thistle

(SOUND CREW 1 strikes triangle.)

STORYTELLER 1:
A fox trotted out in a hungry plight,

(SOUND CREW 2 strikes wood block as FOX trots paws up around the stage.)

STORYTELLER 1:
And begged of the moon to give him light,

(SOUND CREW 5 shakes tambourine as FOX kneels and begs.)

STORYTELLER 1:
For he'd many a mile to trot that night,

(SOUND CREW 2 strikes wood block. FOX trots in little circles.)

STORYTELLER 1:
Before he reached his den...

STORYTELLERS, SOUND CREW & CHORUS *(Throwing hands up, eyes wide.)*
OH!

(SOUND CREW 5 shakes tambourine and slaps it in the center.)

STORYTELLER 2:
And first he trotted to a farmer's yard,

(SOUND CREW 2 strikes wood block as FOX trots and freezes.)

STORYTELLER 2:
Where the ducks and geese's nerves were jarred,

(SOUND CREW 3 and 4 shake rattles as DUCK and GEESE go center shaking.)

STORYTELLER 2:
And their wings were a flapping and their rest was marred

(SOUND CREW 3 and 4 shake rattles vigorously as DUCKS and GEESE flap wings.)

STORYTELLER 2:
By the visit of Mister Fox...

STORYTELLERS, SOUND CREW & CHORUS: *(Throwing hands up, eyes wide.)*
OH!

(SOUND CREW 5 shakes tambourine and slaps it in the center.)

STORYTELLER 3:
He seized the black duck by the neck,
And swung her over across his back;

(SOUND CREW 6 scrapes guiro as FOX mimes throwing DUCK over back.)

STORYTELLER 3:
The black duck cried out, "QUACK! QUACK! QUACK!"

(SOUND CREW 5 honks bike horn as DUCK quacks loudly.)

STORYTELLER 3:
With her legs hanging dangling down.

ALL STORYTELLERS, SOUND CREW & CHORUS: *(Throwing hands up.)*
OH!

(SOUND CREW 5 shakes tambourine and slaps it in the center.)

STORYTELLER 4:
Then Old Mrs. Slipper Slopper jumped out of bed,

(SOUND CREW 2 strikes wood block twice as MRS. SLIPPER SLOPPER jumps.)

STORYTELLER 4:
And out of the window she popp'd her head:

(SOUND CREW 2 strikes wood block twice as MRS. S. pops head forward.)

STORYTELLER 4:
Crying, "John, John, the black duck is gone,

(SOUND CREW 3 and 4 shake maracas vigorously as MRS. S. jumps and waves hysterically.)

STORYTELLER 4:
And the fox is away to his den
STORYTELLERS, SOUND CREW & CHORUS: *(Throwing hands up, eyes wide.)*
OH!"
STORYTELLER 1:
Then, John he ran to the top of the hill,

(SOUND CREW 2 strikes wood block rapidly as JOHN runs breathlessly skidding to a stop. SOUND CREW 5 shakes tambourine and slaps it in the center.)

STORYTELLER 1:
And he blew a blast both loud and shrill;

(JOHN tilts head back and gives mighty blow.)

STORYTELLER 1:
Says the Fox,
FOX: *(Cupping ear.)*
"That is very pretty music; still, I'd rather be home in my den...
STORYTELLERS, SOUND CREW & CHORUS: *(Throwing hands up, eyes wide.)*
OH!"

(SOUND CREW 5 shakes tambourine and slaps it in the center.)

STORYTELLER 2:
At last the fox trotted home to his den,

(SOUND CREW 2 strikes wood block as FOX trots with DUCK beside him in to center.)

STORYTELLER 2:
To his dear little foxes tucked in their pen;

(SOUND CREW 3 and 4 shake maracas and SOUND CREW 6 shakes jingle bells as LITTLE FOXES trot eagerly to center kneeling together.)

STORYTELLER 2:
Says the fox,

FOX: *(Exuberantly raising paw.)*
"You're in luck! Here's a good fat duck,

STORYTELLER 2:
With her legs hanging dangling down.

STORYTELLERS, SOUND CREW & CHORUS: *(Throwing hands up, eyes wide.)*
OH!"

(SOUND CREW 5 shakes tambourine and slaps it in the center.)

STORYTELLER 3:
He then sat down with his hungry wife,

(SOUND CREW 5 shakes tambourine and Sound Crew 6 shake bells as MR. and MRS. FOX hungrily sit.)

STORYTELLER 3:
They never ate better in all their life;

(SOUND CREW 3 and 4 shake maracas as all the FOXES smack lips and lick paws.)

STORYTELLER 3:
And the little ones picked on the bones

(FOXES gnaw the bones enthusiastically.)

STORYTELLERS, SOUND CREW & CHORUS: *(Throwing hands up.)*
OH!

(SOUND CREW 5 shakes tambourine and slaps it in the center. The sung version of the ballad might be performed after the spoken one.)

STORYTELLER 1:
The Eagle

STORYTELLER 1:
By Alfred Lord Tennyson

ACTOR 31:

He clasps the crag with crooked hands;

(SOUND CREW 2 strikes wood block twice as EAGLE clasps crag twice—once with each talon.)

ACTOR 31:

Close to the sun in lonely lands,

(SOUND CREW 5 shakes tambourine. SUN'S arms create high, round SUN.)

ACTOR 31:

Ringed with the azure world, he stands.

(SOUND CREW 1 strikes triangle 3 times. AZURE cloth swirls behind EAGLE and SUN.)

ACTOR 32:

The wrinkled sea beneath him crawls;

(SOUND CREW 6 scrapes guiro as SEA CLOTH wiggles.)

ACTOR 32:

He watches from his mountain walls,

(SOUND CREW 5 shakes tambourine as EAGLE, wings outstretched, peers down.)

ACTOR 32:

And like a thunderbolt he falls.

(SOUND CREW 3 strikes drum firmly. EAGLE shoots arms down as SEA CLOTH is raised perpendicular indicating EAGLE disappearing into sea. EAGLE and SEA CLOTH freeze. SOUND CREW 1 strikes triangle. Actors sit.)

STORYTELLER 2:

America the Beautiful

(SOUND CREW 1 strikes triangle.)

STORYTELLER 2 :
by Katherine Lee Bates

(SOUND CREW 1 strikes triangle.)

STORYTELLER 1:
O beautiful for spacious skies,

(SOUND CREW 1 strikes triangle six times. CHORUS opens arms out creating SKIES. SKIES spread out sky cloth along length of upstage.)

STORYTELLER 2:
For amber waves of grain,

(SOUND CREW 1 strikes triangle as CHORUS sways arms. GRAIN sways floral wheat.)

STORYTELLER 3:
For purple mountain majesties

(SOUND CREW 1 strikes triangle as CHORUS's arms create mountain peaks. PURPLE MOUNTAIN cloth becomes peak.)

STORYTELLER 4:
Above the fruited plain!

(SOUND CREW 1 strikes triangle as CHORUS's arms create TREES bearing fruit. TREE holds out an apple.)

STORYTELLER 1:
America! America!

(SOUND CREW 6 shakes bells as CHORUS wave imaginary flags. FLAG actors wave flags.)

STORYTELLER 2:
God shed His grace on thee

(SOUND CREW 6 shakes jingle bells as CHORUS raise and lower arms prayerfully.)

STORYTELLER 3:

And crown thy good

(SOUND CREW 5 shakes tambourine as CHORUS places imaginary crowns on own heads. STATUE OF LIBERTY forms center stage.)

STORYTELLER 4:

With brotherhood

(SOUND CREW 1 strikes triangle as CHORUS holds hands with person on either side of them.)

STORYTELLER 1:

From sea to shining seas.

(SOUND CREW 1 strikes triangle. CHORUS gestures to one side of the room, and then the other. SOUND CREW 1 strikes triangle.)

("America the Beautiful" is performed twice and perhaps three times. First, the CHORUS recites the song as a poem. Then the CHORUS sings the poem and performs it. After the finale when all performers have been introduced, the audience might join in on a final singing of the patriotic song.)

FINALE

(STORYTELLERS go center stage. They should memorize this part.)

STORYTELLER 1:
Thank you students, adults too.
STORYTELLER 2:
For watching so kindly our show for you
STORYTELLER 3
Of classic poems, old yet new.
STORYTELLER 4:
We hope they came alive for you.
STORYTELLER 1:
And here's a last tip, from us storytellers your friends.
STORYTELLER 2:
Read a book of good poems from beginning to end

STORYTELLER 3:

And memorize poems that you like the best,

STORYTELLER 4:

And you'll find to your life it will add extra zest.

(The STORYTELLERS face the PERFORMERS. Each will announce her or his name loudly and clearly when announced by the STORYTELLERS. SOUND CREW 6 strikes high note on tone bell after each person announces her or his name.)

(STORYTELLERS 1, 2, 3, and 4 facing PERFORMERS and gesturing them to rise when each says their name. They remain standing.)

STORYTELLER 1:

The actors are: *(Name all the actors.)*

STORYTELLER 2:

The sound crew is: *(Name all the sound crew members.)*

STORYTELLER 3 and STORYTELLER 4:

The storytellers are: *(Name all storytellers.)*

ALL STORYTELLERS:

Thank you for coming to our performance.

(STORYTELLERS face actors and raise their arms. PERFORMERS raise their arms with the STORYTELLERS and bring them down together for a bow and sit. "America The Beautiful" might be sung once more with the audience participating.)

PRODUCTION NOTES

The following guidelines may be used to enhance the quality of the production with costumes and props.

COSTUME SUGGESTIONS

For poetry dramatization presentations, all students wear black shirts and black pants with individual character costumes worn as additional pieces to the all-black attire. The costumes should be simple and make a clear immediate statement. STORYTELLERS might wear tunics each of a different color, such as gold, green, blue, and lilac. If storytellers also act, they should wear all black.

SCENE ONE: NONSENSE RHYMES

Humpty Dumpty Sat on a Wall: Beanie or other funny hat, big bright bow tie or other flamboyant tie

Jack Be Nimble: Red nightcap with white tassel (A Santa Claus hat may be adapted.)

Rub-A-Dub-Dub: **Butcher:** White butcher-style apron perhaps left untied
Baker: Tall baker's hat or paper hat used by servers in fast-food restaurants
Candlestick maker: Paul Revere–style tricorner hat.

Old Mother Hubbard: **Mother:** Old-ladyish frilly shower or curler cap of bright color that puffs at the crown and perhaps is decorated with bright artificial flowers, fussy shawl with fringe; **Dog:** Floppy dog ears attached to a baseball cap, head band or elasticized band

Oh, the Grand Old Duke of York: Tall General's military hat—perhaps bright blue with tall red feather. He might wave a tiny flag.

SCENE TWO: LIMERICKS

A Piggish Young Person from Leeds: Black stovepipe hat with pink pig ears of felt or construction paper attached

There Was an Old Man from Peru: Deer-stalker or other eccentric hat and long white beard, a corn cob or other pipe

An Epicure Dining at Crewe: **Male Epicure:** Showy top hat, perhaps silver or gold and matching bow tie; **Female Epicure:** Large hat with tall feathers or too many flowers; **Waiter:** Apron worn hanging down to give a jaunty no-nonsense attitude or bright plaid cummerbund and bow

Higglety, Pigglety, Pop!: **Dog:** Floppy dog ears on a furry cap or beanie; **Pig:** Bright pink beanie or baseball cap worn backwards with pig ears attached; **Cat:** Perky cat ears

Miss Dowd and the Mouse: **Mouse:** Mouse ears; **Miss Dowd:** Spectacles, shawl, pink satin curler cap puffed up at crown with a rosette bow pinned to top

There Was a Young Lady of Niger: **Lady:** Graceful shawl to cover head and shoulders, carrying a large bright fan or a shade umbrella; **Tiger:** Yellow baseball cap with black stripes and yellow-and-black striped tunic

A Flea and a Fly in a Flue: **Flea:** Black baseball cap or visor; **Fly:** Black material draped around shoulders as wings **Flue**: Red or gray fabric—large enough for Flea and Fly to stand behind when held on either side by the Flue actors

SCENE THREE: NATURE POEMS

Windy Nights: **Man**: Tall nineteenth-century black top hat; **Horse**: Black baseball cap with ears attached and black ribbon as a mane

The Wind: No costumes—dramatized through movement

Raindrops: No costumes—dramatized through movement

Silver: Crescent-shaped moon about 12 inches high of stiff cardboard and covered with silver tin foil attached to 3-inch wide elastic band and worn on the head. Blue nylon netting might be attached (representing the sky).

SCENE FOUR: ANIMAL POETRY

How Creatures Move: No costumes—dramatized through movement

The Eagle: White baseball cap with bill colored black with felt tip pen; **Sun**: Gold filmy material tied around the head in a turban or draped over shoulders; **Azure World**: Blue nylon netting (swirled behind sun;) **Wrinkled Sea**: Deep aqua or blue filmy material

Mister Fox: **Mister Fox:** Orange baseball cap with tall fox ears attached and large eyes on either side, orange mittens or gloves; **Black Duck**: Black baseball cap; **Grey Goose**: Grey baseball cap; **Mrs. Slipper Slopper**: Gingham prairie-style bonnet, long apron, spectacles; **John:** Straw farmer's hat, perhaps with grains of wheat sticking up at weird angle; **Mrs. Fox:** Orange baseball cap and orange apron; **Little Foxes:** Orange visors or baseball caps

AMERICA THE BEAUTIFUL FINALE

America the Beautiful: **Skies:** Long blue filmy fabric; **Grain**: Sheaves of wheat. **Mountain:** Purple cloth cut in peaked shape; **Fruited Plain**: Green fabric draped around shoulders, and holding up apple; **Crowned Good**: Gold crown; **Flag Wavers**: Flag for each

Glossary of Drama and Literary Terms

Learning figurative language means hearing poetry's music
and becoming used to its inclinations—its frequent comparisons,
talking to things, its exaggerations, speed, and omniscence.
—Kenneth Koch

alliteration: repetition of consonant sounds, especially at the beginning of words. Examples: The limerick tried to tutor two tooters to toot; "lonely lands" in Alfred Lord Tennyson's *The Eagle*, or in Edgar Allan Poe's *The Raven*, "Doubting, dreaming dreams no mortals ever dared to dream before." Alliteration increases rhythm and creates a musical effect.

apostrophe: address to an absent figure or a thing as if it were present and could hear. Example: Walt Whitman's "O Captain! My Captain!" or William Blake's "Tyger! Tyger! burning bright".

articulation: precise pronunciation of words and syllables using the articulators— jaw, lips, tongue, teeth, and soft palate.

ballad: a song or poem that tells a story. Originally, ballads were composed and sung by anonymous folk singers. Later, authors wrote Literary Ballads that usually aren't sung and that are crafted following the ballad form. Ballads often have short rhyming stanzas of four lines.

blocking: coordination of actors' movement on stage. The director usually plans the blocking with input from actors.

colorization: creating the mood of the language through varying tonal quality, pitch, and gesture.

couplet: a couple or pair of lines of a verse that usually rhyme. Some poems are entirely in rhyming couplets. Examples: *Silver* by Walter De la Mare, "Slowly, silently, now the moon / Walks the night in her silver shoon;" and the poem *A Snowy Day*.

cue: final line or word of one performer's speech signaling the next performer it's her turn to speak.

director: the person responsible for the overall staging of a production. The director coordinates costuming, setting, lighting, music, and sound although these are usually executed by experts. Directors direct the actors and interpret the script.

emphasis: stress on important words (usually verbs or nouns) achieved through variation in volume, pitch, pause, gesture, and facial expression.

figurative language: words used in ways other than the way they are ordinarily used. Thus, *a lemon* is a citrus fruit, but *a lemon* used figuratively means a defective machine. Other examples: "She's a cat," "the wrinkled sea," or the bird's eyes are "like frightened beads." Poetry is notable for imaginative use of language that is not literally true.

free verse: poems with lines of irregular length that usually don't rhyme. Example: "Life for me ain't been no crystal stair./It's had tacks in it, / And splinters, / And boards torn up," from *Mother to Son* by Langston Hughes. The poem *In Just-* by e. e. cummings is another example.

gesture: any movement of the body, arm, head, or face that expresses or emphasizes an idea or emotion. Examples: a threatening or beckoning gesture, a gesture of acceptance or rejection or love, gestures of joy or gloom. Gestures help performers achieve complete communication and intensify the meaning. Enlarged, clear, slow gestures are usually best to dramatize poetry. An indiscriminate use of gestures such as fidgeting detract.

hyperbole: language using great exaggeration, such as Alfred Lord Tennyson describing an eagle as being "close to the sun" or the speaker in William Wordsworth *I Wandered Lonely as a Cloud* seeing "ten thousand daffodils in a glance."

image, imagery: language appealing to the five senses. Examples: "Two roads diverged in a yellow wood," (sight) in Robert Frost's *The Road Not Taken* and "coughing drowns the parson's saw," (hearing) in Shakespeare's "Winter."

inflection: vocal technique in which the voice rises or falls. Rising inflection carries the thought and ideas forward. A falling inflection indicates the end of a thought or idea.

interjection: an exclamation, often of one word, such as Ow! Wow! Good grief! *The Ballad of Mr. Fox* ends each stanza with "Oh!"

internal rhyme: rhyme within the line. Example, the first line of Edgar Allan Poe's *The Raven:* "Once upon a midnight *dreary*, while I pondered weak and *weary.*"

limerick: a humorous five-line verse with an unusual rhyme scheme in which lines one and two rhyme with each other, lines three and four rhyme with each other, and the fifth (or punch line) rhymes with lines one and two.

lyric poetry: poetry expressing emotions or thoughts rather than telling a story. The term comes from ancient Greece where poems were recited to the accompaniment of a lyre, a stringed instrument. Poets now create lyrical poems by using musical poetic devices such as alliteration, rhyme, rhythm, and onomatopoeia. Examples: Walt Whitman's *O Captain! My Captain!* and William Wordsworth's, *I Wandered Lonely as a Cloud.*

metaphor: the comparison of one thing to another without using the words *like* or *as.* Examples: "the wrinkled sea," "Juliet is the sun," "He is a bull in a china shop," "The moon is a silver teacup."

off rhyme or slant rhyme: words that end with similar sounds but do not exactly rhyme. Examples: confirm/perform or might/get. "Pure rhymes" have the feeling of a tight neat completion. Off rhymes are less predictable, adding surprise and complexity to a subject. Example: Many poems by Emily Dickinson use off rhyme.

onomatopoeia: words that sound like what they mean. Examples: *bow wow, snort, clip clop, whoosh, bam, pow, sizzle, hiss.*

pantomime: acting without speaking using facial expression and gesture only.

personification: language in which a non-human thing is given human characteristics, such as "dancing daffodils" in William Wordsworth's *I Wandered Lonely as a Cloud*, an eagle with "crooked hands," in Tennyson's *The Eagle,* or in *Silver* by Walter de la Mare the moon who "walks the night in her silver shoon."

physical stance: body position appropriate to the role—such as a slumped, pulled-in stance for a fearful old man or a statuesque, regal stance for a goddess. A firm stance with hands by the side is appropriate for the recitation of poetry.

pitch: how high or low your voice is. Professional actors usually play parts in their normal range—extending the pitch as much as three octaves when the character, mood, or intensity of the scene requires it.

presentational theatre: acknowledgment by the actors that the audience is "present." In presentational theatre, actors look at the audience and may even interact with them. This differs from realism in which the actors pretend they are carrying on in their own world and the audience doesn't exist. Poetry dramatization and other imaginative literature is usually dramatized in the presentational style.

rate: speed of delivery—e.g., in scenes with quickening hoofbeats, quicken the pace. In death scenes or dreamy pensive states, slow the rate down.

refrain: a repeated phrase, line, or group of lines in songs and poems (especially ballads). Example: "He laid down his hammer and he cried, 'Lord, Lord.' He laid down his hammer and he cried" from *The Ballad of John Henry*. Refrains create a mood and invite an audience to join in.

rhyme: a similarity of sounds between words such as *bright/night, remember / December; frog / bog; moon / spoon/ croon / June.* Rhyme creates delight, aids memory, and helps the words flow easily. It is a kind of word music.It is often found in the early poems and songs of many languages. Early storytellers told rhyming stories to help remember them.

rhyme scheme: the pattern in which rhymes occur in a stanza. Rhyme schemes are represented by giving the same letter of the alphabet to each rhyming word in a stanza. For example: "Double, double toil and trouble; (a) Fire burn and cauldron, bubble. (a) Fillet of a fenny snake (b) In the cauldron boil and bake." (b). This pattern would be called "aabb."

rhythm: repeated and recurrent patterns found everywhere in nature and life that all people respond to. Examples: Day/night, the heart beat's rhythm, and the rise and fall of the tide. Rhythm in poetry is a pattern of stressed and unstressed sounds. For, example in Henry Wadsworth Longfellow's *Paul Revere's Ride*: "Listen, my children, and you shall hear of the midnight ride of Paul Revere" has the rhythm of galloping hoofbeats. Also, repetition of sounds (such as in alliteration) and rhyme can create a rhythm.

run-on line: a line of verse requiring the reader go on to the next line without pausing to understand the meaning. Example: "The cat comes / on little cat feet" from Carl Sandburg's *Fog* or from Emily Dickinson's *A Word,* "I say it just / Begins to live / That day."

script: the text of a play or other spoken performance.

simile: a kind of language making a comparison between two seemingly unlike things using *as, like* or verbs such *as seems*. Examples: William Wordsworth's "I wandered lonely *as a cloud" or* in Langston Hughes *The Negro Speaks of Rivers,* "My soul has grown deep *like the rivers.*"

speaker: the imaginary voice or persona taken by the author of a poem. Thus, the "I" or the person speaking in a poem is not necessarily the author.

stanza: a group of lines forming a unit of thought, similar to a paragraph in prose.

Stanzas often have the same number of lines. Examples: *Uphill* by Christina Rossetti and *The Tyger* by William Blake. Most poems have stanzas.

symbol: a person, object, action, or situation that means more than it literally means. Example: The caterpillar in Christina Rossetti's poem is a caterpillar but also symbolizes our potential to fulfill our most wished-for destinies. The eagle in Tennyson's poem is a bird but it symbolizes proud independence. **Conventional symbols** are those in which people accept that one thing represents another. Example: The American flag represents the United States of America.

tempo: how fast or slowly you speak.

tercet: A triplet or stanza of three lines in which each line ends with the same rhymes. Example: *The Eagle* by Alfred Lord Tennyson.

tone: the feeling of a work that is created by the author's choice of words and details (i.e., joyful, serious, sad, thoughtful, mysterious, sarcastic, playful). Examples: *Fog* by Carl Sandburg is mysterious. *Caterpillar* by Christina Rossetti is thoughtful; *The Ballad of Mr. Fox* is comical.

verse: language that usually uses rhythm and rhyme. Verse is a broader category than serious poetry and includes verse such as that in greeting cards or chanted by children on playgrounds.

vocal variety: using as many speaking techniques as needed to convey all of a poem's meaning.

vocal quality: whether your voice is shrill, nasal, raspy, lilting, simpering, booming.

volume: loudness or softness of voice. Varying the volume can convey subtle dramatic meanings. For example, recite the first line of line "Double, double toil and trouble" softly and the following line, "Fire burn and cauldron bubble" loudly to create a surprising menace.

Subject Index Across the Curriculum

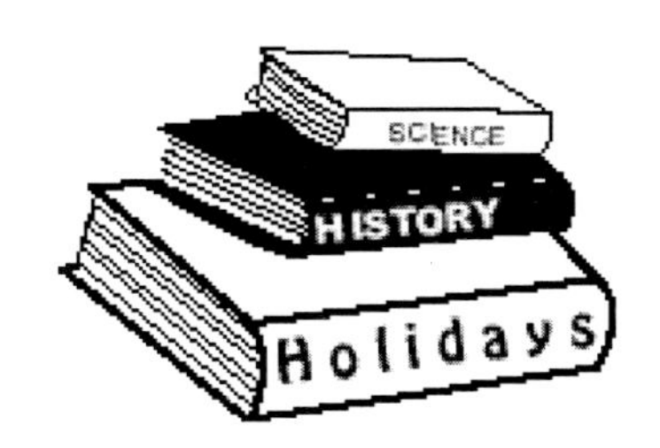

Art brings us together as a family.
It comes from the part of us without fear, prejudice, and malice.
—Jessye Norman, opera singer

Index of Authors, Titles, and First Lines

A poet is above all else, a person who is passionately in love with language.
—W. H. Auden

Selected Bibliography

Literature is a big sea full of many fish.
I put down my nets and pull. I'm still pulling.
—Langston Hughes

RESOURCES ON POETRY

Barnet, Sylvan, Morton Berman, William Burto and William E. Cain. *An Introduction to Literature. 11th ed.* Longman, 1997. Impressive collection of poems, stories, and plays with insightful, clear, discussion of the works, and questions on the works and literary techniques.

Hirsch, E. D. Jr. *The Dictionary of Cultural Literacy.* Boston: Houghton Mifflin, 1987. Helpful reference including many poems dramatized in this book and other literary-historical information that the author believes Americans should know to be culturally aware citizens.

Koch, Kenneth. *Rose, Where Did You Get That Red? Teaching Great Poetry to Children.* New York: Random House, 1973. Inspiring and practical book describing how to teach students how to write poetry by studying the poetry of such classic authors as William Blake, William Shakespeare, Walt Whitman, Samuel Taylor Coleridge, Federico García Lorca, and others.

Koch, Kenneth and Kate Farrell. *Talking to the Sun: An Illustrated Anthology of Poems for Young People.* New York: The Metropolitan Museum of Art and Holt, Rinehart and Winston, 1985. This inviting book with poems illustrated by European, American, and Japanese art will inspire students to create art to illustrate poems.

Sullivan, Charles, editor. *Imaginary Gardens: American Poetry and Art for Young People.* New York: Harvey N. Abrams, Inc., 1989. Cartoons, fine art, photos, and graphics illustrate American poems. Includes *Paul Revere's Ride* with John Singleton Copley's portrait of Paul Revere and pictures of Walt Whitman and Edgar Allan Poe.

ACTING

Bruder, Melissa. *A Practical Handbook for the Actor.* New York: Vintage Originals, 1986. Clear basic acting book. Valuable to both beginning and advanced acting students.

McGaw, Charles. *Acting is Believing: A Basic Method.* Seventh Edition. Harcourt Brace, 1995. Clear and practical with acting exercises that will interest drama students in high school and advanced acting students.

DIRECTING

Busti, Kathryn Michele. *Stage Production Handbook.* Littleton, Colo.: Theatre Things, 1992. Step-by-step guidelines and checklists to copy for students on every technical aspect of putting on a show. Arranged in convenient, tabbed, three-ring binder. Valuable resource for teachers and students producing a play.

Clurman, Harold. *On Directing.* Simon and Schuster, 1997. Entertaining, clear book by a master director on all aspects of directing a play.

Hodge, Francis. *Play Directing: Analysis, Communication and Style*, fourth edition, Prentice Hall, 1994. Thorough account of all aspects of directing a play. Of value to the novice and the advanced director.

McCullough, L.E. *Anyone Can Produce Plays with Kids: The Absolute Basics of Staging Your Own At-Home, In-School, 'Round the Neighborhood Plays.* Lyme, N.H.: Smith and Kraus, Inc., 1998. A complete guide for parents or teachers with little or no drama background. Teaches the basics of playmaking: organizing a group of children, selecting a script, assembling costumes and props, running rehearsals, handling technical aspects of production and promotion, and directing.

COSTUMES

Hershberger, Priscilla. *Make Costumes for Creative Play*. Danbury, Conn.: Grolier Educational Corporation, 1993. Imaginative simple costumes with clear instructions. Includes, for example, a tiger headdress made with an orange hand towel marked with felt tip pen and headbands using fabric trim. Wonderful color illustrations show how to make the costumes.

MUSICAL INSTRUMENTS

West Music Company, 1212 5th Street, Coralville, Iowa 52241 (1-800-397-9378). A very complete catalogue of reasonably priced instruments. Also has books on teaching music and movement, silk scarves, and other materials helpful in dramatizing the poetry in this book.

Fiarotta, Noel and Phyllis Fiarotta. *Music Crafts for Kids—The How-To Book of Music Discovery*. New York: Sterling Publishing Company, Inc., 1993. A charming book with a variety of information on music and the creation of simple instruments. Both students and teachers will enjoy this book.

LITERATURE DRAMATIZATION

Thistle, Louise. *Dramatizing Aesop's Fables.* Lyme N.H.: Smith and Kraus, Inc., 1993. Aesop's Fables dramatized for the classroom or use on the stage. Includes acting techniques, character warm-ups, and critical-thinking questions.

Thistle, Louise. *Dramatizing Three Classic Tales—The Three Billy Goats Gruff, The Little Red Hen, and The Lion and the Mouse.* Lyme, N.H.: Smith and Kraus, Inc., 1999. Three tales dramatized with action pictures, suggested gestures, and "chant" words to say and do to develop language and to involve students completely in the stories. (Available in English and Spanish versions.) Recommended for language learners of English and Spanish. Older students might perform these for younger ones.

Thistle, Louise. *Dramatizing Mother Goose*. Lyme, N.H.: Smith and Kraus, Inc., 1998. Seventeen Mother Goose rhymes scripted to dramatize in the classroom and on stage. Costume and rhythm instrument suggestions, literature questions, and historical background on Mother Goose. Use as an introduction to the study of nonsense verse and to performance for younger students.

Thistle, Louise. *Dramatizing Myths and Tales*. Lyme N.H.: Smith and Kraus, Inc., 1995. Myths and tales dramatized from five cultures: West African, Mayan, Native American, Japanese, and British Isles. Includes detailed description of how to cast and direct beginning acting students in a play.